A wise man endeavours

A man that knows how to

A woman and a glass are never out of Danger.
A good servant disputeth not his masters Command,
                         But doeth it.
Be just, But trust not every one.
Be slow in chusing a friend, But slower in changing.
Be always more ready to forgive than to return
                         an Injury.
By good nature half the misery of Human life
                         might be Assuaged.
Betray no trust: Divulge no Secret.
Believe not all you hear and report not all
                         you Believe
Bear your misfortunes with Fortitude
Beware to whom you commit the secrets of
                         your Mind.
Be ready to hear, Careful to Contrive and
                         Slow to Advise.
Be not too hasty to outbid Another.
Beware of the Geese when the fox Preaches.
Better are small fish than an empty dish.
Bad as it is to be fawned upon it is better
                         than to be Bitten
Better to slip with the foot than the Tongue
By doing nothing we learn to do Ill.
Be as careful of the property of others as you
                         would your Own
Be active, for Idleness is the rust of the
                         Mind.

To Grandfathers past and present

A Bradwell Man

Cheetham William Fletcher, 3 January 1894 to 31 October 1943

A Bradwell Man

Inspired by the writing of Cheetham W Fletcher,
a Peak District Village Joiner
(1894 to 1943)

Barry & Bill Fletcher

High Peak Books - Hope Valley - England

First published in Great Britain 1998
by High Peak Books
10 The Dale, Hathersage
Hope Valley S32 1EQ
© 1998 Barry & Bill Fletcher
All rights reserved.
No part of this publication may be
reproduced or transmitted in any form
or by any means without permission.
ISBN 0 9532342 0 7
Printed in Great Britain by
The Peak Press Company
Chapel-en-le-Frith
High Peak SK23 9RQ

CONTENTS

		Page
	Acknowledgements	viii
	Introduction	ix
Chapter 1	Early Years	11
Chapter 2	The First World War (1914-18)	27
Chapter 3	Between the Wars	59
Chapter 4	Second World War including The Bradwell Home Guard	93
Chapter 5	Further Poems with Jokes and Tales from Bradwell and roundabout	135
Chapter 6	The last few months	153
Chapter 7	Reflections by Bill Fletcher	159
Chapter 8	Reflections on the writing of this book	163

Appendices

1	Family Tree	187
2	Sketch map of the area showing places referred to by Cheet'	188
3	Bradwell village walks calling at main places associated with Cheet'	189
4	List of key dates before, during and after Cheet's life	194
5	List of illustrations	197
6	Bibliography	200
	Index	201

ACKNOWLEDGEMENTS

Heartfelt thanks go to the following people for their invaluable contributions to this book:

Shirley Archer; Chris Blantern; Bill Bough; Jack & Helen Bough; Tom Buxton; Chesterfield Library (Local Studies Section); Clifford Cockayne; Wilf & Dorothy Cushworth; Peter & Jean Davies; Derbyshire Records Office, Matlock; Andrew Ferrill; Miss H. E. Fischer; Ian Flemming; Anita Fletcher; Brian (Nat) & Pam Fletcher; Jackie Fletcher; Joan Fletcher; Joyce Fletcher; Mark Fletcher; May Fletcher; Ned & Sheila Fletcher; Noel & Freda Fletcher; Eric Gill; Mike & Cynthia Grayson; Eileen Hancock; Annie Hartle; Cliff Housley, Regimental Historian, The Sherwood Foresters; Ken and Barbara Marples; David Megginson; Robert Mulholland of Peak Press; Marjorie Nunn; Paul O'Mahony; George Parritt; Sheffield City Library (Local Studies Section); Marian Smith of Bakewell Register Office; Harry White; Mike Whittaker.

INTRODUCTION

Cheetham William Fletcher, 'Cheet' to those who knew him, was born in January 1894 in the Peak District village of Bradwell. After leaving school and trying two jobs Cheet' went to work for his father, John, who had started a local business as joiner, wheelwright and undertaker. In 1914, along with a couple of his friends, he enlisted in the Sherwood Foresters and following basic training arrived in France in February 1915. In December of that year he was wounded and brought back to England in January 1916. He returned to France in the following June, a mere two days after his marriage to Grace, and apart from occasional leave there he stayed until the end of the war in December 1918.

Twenty years later he was to be touched again by war and he played a full and active part in Home Guard duties in and around the Hope Valley. In 1937 he began to compile a hand written journal using a cash book into which he entered diaries, stories, jokes, poems and sayings. Six years later he would die peacefully in his sleep, but his journal would survive as a permanent reminder of a man who, despite being well known, liked and respected, was often described as a character, a joker and a prankster.

Cheet' wrote vividly and poignantly of his experiences in the latter part of WWI, at the time of the breaking of the Hindenberg Line, including the sudden, premature losses of newly-made friends. His razor-sharp perception of people and events around him shines through in his writing. A lively style of wit and humour is used to describe village characters and events and this is contrasted by his matter-of-fact reporting of the starkness of war.

More than 50 years after his death Cheet's writing has been combined with facts, memories, stories and pictures to provide a rich insight into his life and times. With its blend of autobiography and biography this book includes the full contents of his journal, some other fragments of his writing and supporting information from other sources. 'A Bradwell Man' also describes some of the thoughts and feelings generated by the writing of the book.

Throughout the book a special typeface has been reserved for Cheet's writing; for example:

> *Courage ought to have eyes as well as arms.*
> *Credit not him whose tongue speaketh wonders.*
> *Counsels in wine seldom prosper.*
> *Cloudy mornings often bring clear evenings.*
> *Clowns are fit company only for their fellows.*

CHAPTER 1
EARLY YEARS

"My Life Story by C W Fletcher"

When I start this tale I am 46 years of age and now some people say I was such a devil I ought never to have been born. I don't know that I ever did anybody any real harm, only I was always full of fun, etc. I was born in Bradwell, in a cottage up Far Hill. I could never do anything right for my Father, as far as I can remember.

When I was quite a nipper I used to go up to Hannah Hibbs, who kept a shop just above where we lived. I would wrap a stone in paper, as if my Mother had wrapped me a halfpenny up, to buy some sweets with, and then go up to Hannah's for a halfpenny worth of sweets. She would serve me then I would leave her shop, after putting the stone wrapped in paper on the counter of course she got wide to that.

There was another shopkeeper, the name of Josephine, who kept a shop where Roberts bakehouse is now . . she was shortsighted. I used to wrap a farthing up in silver paper ever so neatly then go to her shop for a pennyworth of sweets and get fivepence change. I remember once I was missed by my Mother. I was found in Albert Palfreyman's shop. Wasn't I having a time what with fruit and sweets etc, I think I had nibbled everything in the shop. My didn't I get tanned when they found me.

As a young boy I had to go to Chapel . . didn't I put some buttons in the collecting box after I had spent the halfpenny.

We used to sit up in what we called the Gods. They were the back seats in the Gallery. When the preacher was praying we used to take our pea shooters out of our pockets and then the fun began. Many a time has old William Bradwell or Bill Swift turned us out of Chapel.

Nearly every night we used to go out plaguing people. Old Luther Cooper who lived up Hill Head, we nearly drove him dotty. He got a dog to frighten us, that made us go all the more. We called him the Duke. We used to sly up to his door and stamp on the step or knock at the door. He then would come out and run us. We used to go out window tapping . . we had some fun with that game, you never see it done now. Then there was Bobby Brown: we all knew him, couldn't he use the stick. We used to split the gang up into two lots, one lot would be waiting at Emma Evans chip shop at the Town Bottom, the other part of the gang would be waiting at John Hall's corner. When P C Brown came on duty the gang at Hall's corner would put their fingers in their mouths and start whistling for all they were worth. Brown would start after them, then we would follow on and we would start whistling. Poor old Brown, he didn't know what to do, but he never summonsed us, but he used his stick heavy.

I remember one night the gang was going up Smalldale. I was a bit in front of the others, so I got a handful of stones unbeknown to the other lads. When I got to Marshall Elliotts Father's house I let go with my handful of stones and broke both glass panels in the door. Someone told who it was and I had to replace them.

One Xmas mischief night we were taking gates etc off, we got on top lanes and someone said lets take old Ash's gate off. Something told me not to touch it, so I said no leave it old Ash might be waiting for us. So we left it alone, next day Mr Ash came to our house. Yes he says, it's a good job you didn't take my gate away last night, I was waiting behind the gate, if you had have touched it I should have broken your fingers with my stick, I was waiting for you.

We had a fine Gang. Names were Myself, George Slater, Arthur Maltby, Frank Roe Middleton, Frank Liversedge, Charles Andrew, George Walker, Charles Ross and Frank Palfreyman.

We were a rum lot I can tell you. We used to be in someone's orchard every night in the season, and it wasn't very often we were caught. One Sunday we were up Bradwell Dale rocks throwing stones down on old John Wragg's building. It had a corrugated iron roof and we broke the roof in and broke one shaft off his trap. Bobby Brown came and climbed up the rocks and fetched us out of a cave and took us nearly to Castleton to the lock up but he let us go again of course we had to pay for the damage done.

Another game of ours was to look out for running taps, then we would go and stuff the outlet of the sink pipe with rags and paper; of course the old stone sinks had no overflow and you can imagine what a mess the people had next morning with water all over the floor. Another trick we used to do was look out for a handy chimney, one with plenty of smoke coming out on a cold winter's night. Then we would get a Clod and put it solid on the chimbney, my didn't the house used to get full of Smoke and the people in the House couldn't recon up what was the Matter.

We had some queer old Cronies in those days. Old Joe Cuckoo or Joe Hallam. We used to shout cuckoo after him. He once told me if he could get hold of me he would rub my nose in the ground till I had none. Another old cronie was William Oldfield. We named him Cock layer. I think he would have Brained us if he could have caught us. Then there was Albert Elliott. I remember when he lived in Hollow Gate. His wife used to leave her Bucket outside the door on a stone slab night after night. I would go and kick the bucket down the street. Mr Elliott told me many a time when I was Grown up that he had waited for me night after night to try and catch me. But he never did.

One Xmas Eve we went on the Fields to throw old Hibbertson Middleton's Traps in the Brook. We got the Traps to the Gate and found two big Chains padlocked round the Gate and Stoop. Not to be beaten I slipped off to the workshop, got Hammers and chisels and cut the chain links. Then we threw the traps in the brook. Well Hibbertson said it was me, as nobody else would have thought of Cutting the links.

I remember one day I was stood on the Bridge and the young Men dared me to go and kick at old Bobby Brown's door, of course I went and didn't I kick the door, old Brown dashed out without his Tunic or hat and followed me up as far as the White Hart. Didn't he slash me a few days after with his stick.

One night myself and Cyril Evans were having a walk and I had two Glass Bottles in my hand. What's the bottles for says Cyril. Ho I says I will show you a trick Shortly when we got up to little Sammies, Nurse Middletons Husbands they had

Glass panels in their door. I got a large stone, threw it at the door, and dashed the two Bottles on the Flags. Of course I ran and left Cyril in the lurch and didn't he cop it.

I was coming down Smalldale one night the snow was on the Ground and Tants door was open, so I gently went up to the door and peeped in. They were having supper. I made about half a dozen good Snowballs, then I threw them all on the Table. You should have seen Tants lot after me, of course they put it in the police hands, But never found out.

We used to go up to little Hucklow when it was the Sermons, we knew of a good Orchard. This Sunday night we went up and when the people had gone into chapel we thought we would attend to the orchard. Frank Liversedge was first over the orchard fence, and he dropped above the knees into a Trench filled with night Soil. Poor Frank he had a new suit of Clothes on, his first long Trousers. Well we came back and we had to wash his Trousers in a dam. Of course we couldn't make a very good job of them, But when his Mother had washed them they Shrank that much that he had to wear them as short Trousers. Didn't he get Spanked, I was glad it wasn't me.

Many a time we used to fasten the people in the House while we raided the Gardens. Poor old Fish Tenter Ashton, we used to Torment him to Death catching his Trout. He once told my Uncle Ben, There's only one Lad I want to catch and thats that Fletcher Lad. Of course it didn't make any difference we kept catching his Trout. He nearly caught us several times. We once ran in a Fowl House and he walked round it, but as luck would have it he didn't look inside.

I remember one day I went up to feed the cattle and I had an empty sweet Bag with me so I three part filled the Bag with new Sheep Droppings. Coming down on my way to School I called at Liversedges, and holding the Bag of Sheep droppings in front of Mrs Liversedge who was short sighted, I said will you have a sweet Mrs. I, she says, what sort are they. Hot ones. Of course she took two or three and when she had tasted, I had to clear out quick.

We one night dropped an old dead Fowle down Mrs Ross Chimbney. She played the devil and had the police up. Of course it wasn't us.

Another trick was the parcel trick. My Father went out and Shot a Hare for Xmas, I got all the inside of the Hare and made such a lovely parcel, then planted it in Hollow Gate ready for the people going to early Morning Service. In a bit down comes Mrs Ellen Wood, Nurse Middleton and Frances. Of course Ellen spots the parcel, puts it under her Cape and she admitted she never heard the Service, for wondering what would be in the parcel. I wonder what she thought when she did arrive home and unfasten the parcel. I have done dozens of tricks like this.

Many a time we have been and changed peoples washing. Took it off one line and put it on someone else's and changed over. I bet the people's eyes used to pop out of their heads when they saw someone else's washing on their lines.

About once a week we used to wait for Hibbertson Middleton coming home with his pony and Trap. Sometimes we would lay in wait up Bradwell Dale. When he arrived we would dash out and all pull Back behind his Trap. Of course we could pull his old pony to a standstill. Then old Hibbertson would let the Sparks fly with his Whip.

We used to like a pot sale at Town Bottom, then we would pin old papers on the Goody Goody people's back. 5th of November night, the Bradwell people used to dread it. I remember being at a House and the Builders were putting a new Floor in the Basement. A Bad Tempered old Joker was watching them at work and it was going dusk. I thought now for some fun. I had some fireworks in my pocket, so I got a long piece of String and went upstairs to a window above where this old Joker was stood. Tying a firework onto the string I let it down behind the old man. It made a big Bang and the old man jumped about a foot in the air. I repeated the same joke about half a dozen times.. The old man cursed and Raved, he could not find out who was doing it, and it was a good job he didn't find out, or I believed he would have killed me. He never could take a Joke.

We used to go and tease old Henry Hill who lived near the old Chapel. One night we went as usual and Kicked at his door. My word out he came with a big red hot poker in his hand, swearing vengeance and that he would Brand us for life if he could catch us. He nearly caught me, missed me by an hair's Breadth. We called him Red Hot potter ever after. He scared me that night, I thought my end was near.

One night we had been on the Hills teasing people and we had thrown a stone at Snuffling John's door, John Bradwell. I was trotting down Church Street being the last among my pals.

When I got onto the Bridge Lena Hall says, Who are you plaguing now. Only old Jack Bradda says I. Well he happened to be her uncle and of course she told him who I was. When I got home there was Mr Bradwell sat in the Corner. Anyway I got out of the scrape with telling a lot of Lies. But didn't he curse and swear at me.

We fastened old John Palfreyman in the Shippon one night and he had to stay in from about 7 o'clock until after Eleven. He would not have got out then only his daughter went to see what was wrong.

Three old Ladies were sat on the Bath Seat one night. I put an old White Sheet on and reared up behind them. You could not see them for dust running up to Bradwell. Old Brown got on the War path next day. I had nearly frightened the old dames out of their wits, poor old Ladies.

One dark wet night I was leaving work and Billy Elliott was stood under Emma Chips window. Come with me Bill, says I. Of course Billy would be Ten years older than me. Where are you going says Bill. Well I used to go under the Wesleyan School a lot in those days and there was a small door on the chapel side you could unfasten with a Bolt from the inside. Well this night, that I asked Billy to go with me, they were having a meeting in the Schoolroom. Anyway I got Bill to go with me. When I got him underneath the school I said have you any matches, so he lent me his matches, which I wanted so as I could leave him in the dark.. Then I got a large block of wood and started Bump, Bump, Bumping the floor above me. When I thought I had done enough I dashed through the small door and came to watch what they would do to poor Bill. Well Dennis Evans, Jack Dixon and a few more raced down and under the School. Out they brings William, kicking him and pulling his ears. It isn't me he was shouting, it's Cheet Fletcher. Anyway it was him they had got and he had to have the Blame. Poor old Bill he was after me for weeks but I was always too Smart for him. Nobody could ever get Bill to go with them again. Wasn't it a trick to play on anyone.

I Worked for my Father when I left School. Of course, first I worked a few weeks at Bamford Mill. I didn't like that, so my Father took me to work at Cravens of Darnall, to learn carriage Building. I wasn't there very long and my Father started a Business of his own, in Bradwell, as Joiner, Wheelwright and Undertaker etc and I worked with him, of course we had a small farm as well. I could never do anything right for him, never. If I went to feed the Fowles, I had always not given them enough to eat, or too much, same with the cattle.

I used to have to be up at six o'clock in the morning, and I never hardly finished before eight or Nine at Night. I never had a weeks Holiday, up to going in the Army, except at my Grandfathers, who lived at Peak Forest, and I had to work harder there than at home, because they had a bigger farm and also a Wheelwrights Shop.

I never dare tell my Father when I had broken a wood chisel, or Brace Bit, or any other tool, I used to bury it in the Shop Yard then it was never found. I had a very hard life I can tell you. I never could make a good enough job when I was at my trade, how I tried it was always a damn rotten Job. When I was 20 *years of age I was getting 3 pence a Week pocket money from my Father, and 3 pence from my Mother unbeknown to my Father.*

I wonder what a young man would do today if his parents gave him sixpence a week pocket money. Today they get five or six Shillings to spend each week. Today there is too much going off, such as the pictures, Dancing and Whist drives etc. Then now adays a lad starts smoking and courting nearly as soon as he leaves school. I dare not Smoke in the house when I was Twenty years of age. Still we used to make our own enjoyments. We were always full of fun.

Cheetham William Fletcher (Cheet') was born on 3 January 1894 to John and Annie Fletcher. Annie's maiden name was Hallam and, coming from a strong 'chapel' family in Bradwell, her marriage service to John was probably at the Wesleyan chapel. Cheet' was almost certainly named after Annie's father, Cheetham William Hallam. Seth Evans's fine book "Methodism in Bradwell" includes a photograph of a group of teachers in 1866, one of whom is Cheetham William Hallam. The latter had been named after William Cheetham, a fervent Methodist and the first postmaster of Bradwell.

Early photographs of John, Annie and their family are taken outside Rock Hill Cottage, Far Hill, which points to this as Cheet's birthplace. His birth certificate simply gives Bradwell as his place of birth and lists his father John as a Joiner (Journeyman). John and his two younger brothers, Tom and Bill, were joiners and as young men they worked at Buxton Lime Firms, which became Imperial Chemical Industries in 1931.

Outside Rock Hill cottage; circa 1900. From left to right: Cheet', John, Constance Ann, Annie and Jack.

Cheet', Jack and Colin outside Rock Hill cottage; circa 1905

John's family had a long history in Peak Forest and in all probability was descended from Francis Fletcher of Dam Dale who was born around 1695. Cheet's cousin Ned, born in 1926, lives at Dam Dale Farm, Peak Forest with his wife Sheila and this is the farm to which Cheet' went on working holidays as a young man. This was the home of his grandparents, John Fletcher and Sarah Ann (born Ashton).

Dam Dale Farm, Peak Forest; taken 1950 but little changed since 1900

The last will and testament of Cheet's great grandfather, another John Fletcher, throws extra light on the family's history. The original will is in the possession of Ned and Sheila Fletcher and its contents are reproduced below:

"This is the last will and testament of me John Fletcher of Peak Forest in the County of Derby farmer made and published as follows first I order and direct that all my just debts funeral expenses and the proving and executing of this my will will be paid and discharged by my executors hereinafter named and appointed from and out of my personal estate and effects with all convenient speed after my decease and subject thereto I dispose of my property as follows that is to say I give and bequeath the goodwill of the farm one cow and one stack of hay in the dale to my son

John Fletcher and give and bequeath my farming implements stock household goods and furniture hay all my personal estate and effects wheresoever and whatsoever to be equally divided amongst my eight children Benjamin Fletcher Thomas Fletcher William Fletcher John Fletcher James Fletcher Ann Taylor Vernon Mary Lomas Hannah Fletcher share and share alike and lastly I appoint my son John Fletcher and my son in law Thomas Taylor Vernon executors of this my will and I do declare this to be and contain my last will and testament in witness whereof I the said John Fletcher do set my hand and seal this first day of November in the year of our Lord one thousand eight hundred and seventy seven signed and declared by this said John Fletcher the testator to be his last will and testament in the presence of us who at his request and in his presence and in the presence of each other have subscribed our names as witnesses".

The will bears the signatures of William Critchlow and Francis Fletcher, both of Peak Forest.

John and Annie Fletcher had four further children in addition to Cheet'. Two girls, Sarah Annie and Constance Ann were short lived and died at the ages of two years eight months and three years two months respectively. Cheet's daughter-in-law, Joyce, who now lives in Wales recalled that Annie once told her "we couldn't rear girls". Cheet's two brothers, John (Jack) and Colin were born in 1895 and 1900.

Referring to some of the people and places mentioned in Cheet's journal, Josephine's shop, latterly Roberts' bakehouse, is situated at the bottom of Towngate and is now a bookmakers.

The Chapel to which Cheet' refers is Bradwell Methodist Church, situated on Towngate. Bobby Brown served as Bradwell Police Constable for more than 30 years. He lived in Church Street, opposite Brook Buildings, and retired sometime after World War I.

Amongst his fellow gang members Cheet' mentions Arthur Maltby, Frank Roe Middleton, George Walker and Charles Ross. In Bradwell Churchyard is to be found the War Memorial which lists "The men of this parish who fell in the Great War". Listed amongst the 33 casualties are the names A Maltby, F R Middleton, G Walker and C S Ross.

John Hall's corner is in the immediate vicinity of Bradwell's Ice Cream shop which is near the 'Bridge' where the main road crosses Bradwell Brook in between Netherside and Church Street. The 'Bath Seat' would have been in the vicinity of the old Bath Hotel.

Bamford Mill is on the River Derwent at the bottom of Bamford village. Cheet's wife to be, Grace Pember Bough, worked there for a time as a millhand and this could have been where they first met. For some years the mill was the home of the Carbolite company before being converted to private dwellings in the 1990s. Cravens of Darnall would almost certainly be the forerunner of Cravens Homalloy, an engineering firm on Staniforth Road, Darnall, Sheffield which Cheet's grandson Barry used to visit in the late 1960s.

John Fletcher started his joinery business in the brookside building which later became the Constitutional Club and in the 1950s the meeting place for Bradwell Cub Scouts. The building is in full view to anyone standing on the 'Bridge' and facing downstream. John Fletcher's 'small farm' was situated behind the dwellings on the left hand side of the road which links Far Hill, through Dialstones, to Hill Head.

John Fletcher's workshop at The Butts, Bradwell

*Fletcher's,
Signwriters, Joiners, Wheelwrights,
Undertakers and Decorators,
The Butts, Bradwell,
Via Sheffield.*

Early Business Card

As a young man, Cheet' in Sunday best clothes; circa 1912

This is an appropriate place to introduce William Bough, Cheet's future father-in-law. Born in 1850, William lived in the village of Derwent which during the 1940s was to be lost forever with the construction of Ladybower reservoir. He and his wife had two sons, Billy and Harry, and a daughter Grace Pember who was to marry Cheet' in 1916. Pember was the maiden name of their mother who came from Norton, Sheffield. Harry left school around 1910, and he worked on the construction of the Howden and Derwent reservoirs which came into use in 1912 and 1916 respectively.

William Bough aged 52 years, Cheet's future father-in-law; 1902

Cheet's daughter-in-law, Joyce Fletcher, explained that William Bough had been a member of the Royal Canadian Mounted Police force. Later he pursued his trade as a stonemason and, being ambidextrous, was in popular demand. Annie Fletcher's brothers, Alf and Ben, were stonemasons and they knew Grace's father by reputation as a top class stonemason. William was a journeyman and buildings upon which he worked included Liverpool cathedral and Sheffield Town Hall which was completed in 1897.

Chapter 2
The First World War (1914-18)

I always wanted to Join the army so when War broke out in 1914, I thought it a very good chance to get there so on the 7th September 1914, myself, Percy Bradwell, and Lionel Middleton, walked to Hope Station and went to Sheffield. My parents didn't know anything about my going, I just vanished, and I didn't write for Weeks.

In those days the roads wernt Ashfelted, they where limestone roads & when you walked on them they used to Splash your trouses, when it had rained. Anyway when we got to Sheffield, we went to what they called the Jungle & there where scores of men lined Up waiting to enlist, so I thought, Im not waiting here, in this que, So we went straight up to the door, with much Grumbling amongst the other men, A policeman stood each side the door, & one of them said, you three get to the back & wait your turn. I said to him, I think these men wont mind us three getting in to enlist before them, as you can see by our Trouses that we have walked from out of Derbyshire & we would like to get back before dark, that did the trick, in we went & all three passed A.1.

Next day they sent us to Derby Barracks, We stayed a few weeks at Derby & the policemen drilled us. From Derby they Transfered us to a place called Backworth. We where under Canvas, We stayed at Backworth a few Weeks, then we where moved to Whitley Bay & Billetted us in the Espanade and Waverley Hotels, We enjoyed every minuit of our Time at Whitley the people were so good to us, I have marched a few hundred times round the Band Stand at Whitley Bay.

While in Whitley Bay, I was always on defaulters doing C.B. I have seen when I have done 10 days C.B & then broke Bounds, and had another 14 Days on Top. Our Major who used to sentence us had a Glass Eye, But by Gosh he knew me. I remember fighting one night in one of the Bedrooms, in the Esplanade Hotel. I was 14 Stone then the other chap Tom Foster by name, he came from Mickelover Nr. Derby a Chap older than me but about 16 Stone, I dont know which of us was getting the worst of it, (I think I was) when all at once the door flew open & three of our Cooks came in to the room they where covered with white plaster, They had been sleeping in the room underneath ours, & with fighting the Cieling had fallen in on top of the three Cooks, I think myself and Foster got 21 days C.B.

We used to patrol from Whitley Bay to Tynemouth each night, in out turns, looking for lights in the houses or anything that looked suspicious. After we had trained at Whitley Bay for a few weeks, they moved us to Tynemouth We billited in the Grand Hotel, After Staying at Tynemouth for a few weeks they took us back to Whitley Bay.

In Feb, 1915 they came round for Volunteers for France, I think every man Volunteered But they only wanted 30, I was one of the picked Lads to go. They fitted us out with Kit, & we Sailed from Southampton the same month and arrived at Boulyne France. The Morning after our arrival we where inspected by a General, After he had inspected us, He told us we were not half trained, and that we should have to have a fortnight on the Bull Ring. My God, I Shall never forget it, we had to get up a five Oclock in the Mornings & we drilled until

Dark, in Sand over our Shoe Tops, you should have seen the men drop down in faints etc Our instructers rode on Horse Back.

Five months after arriving in France Cheet' sent an embroidered card with the message "Liberty and Homeland" to his younger brother Colin, then aged fourteen. On it he wrote:

July 21st/1915 from Cheet To Colin With best Love XXXXX
Dear Colin
Just a line to thank you for the Cigs & Cig Case hoping this finds you all well at home as it leaves me in the Pink. Tell them all I am in the best of health from C.W. XXX

Embroidered card to youngest brother Colin

As a consequence of being in France, Cheet' and Grace's courtship was interrupted. A Post Card from Grace to Cheet', postmarked "Bradwell, Sheffield, 19 September 1915" and addressed to "Private C W Fletcher, No 15428, Sherwood Foresters, B Company, British Expeditionary Force, France. c/o G P O London" must have reached its destination. Her message read:

"Dear Cheet
    Just a line hoping you are in the best of health & spirits as it leaves me at present. Hoping you have received my letters. Received your letter & Brooch was very pleased. Will write letter in week so no more now With best love From Grace Be careful & good Luck
I L Y A   XXXXX"

Grace with ornate window in background

Post Card from Grace to Cheet; 19 September 1916

Looking relaxed, Cheet' and colleague in uniform, bareheaded

Cheet' and colleague in Tin Hat

Cheet', standing back row right, with six colleagues

The Derbyshire Courier of Saturday 1 January 1916, in its column headed "This Week's List of Casualties" bore the news that Private C Fletcher of Bradwell had been wounded. A short accompanying story with the heading "Bradwell Man's Bullet Wound" went on to say "Mr John Fletcher, joiner, Bradwell , has received notification by field card that his son, Cheetham Fletcher, has been wounded in action, and is now in hospital somewhere in France. A further communication stated that he had been wounded in the chest and shoulder by a bullet, but that the bullet had been successfully removed."

Two weeks later, the Courier of 15 January 1916, under the heading "Bradwell Casualties" carried the following story: "Private Cheetham W. Fletcher (York and Lancs), of Bradwell, who, as announced in last week's Courier, has been wounded in the chest by a bullet which has now been extracted, expects soon to be sent to England to recuperate." Cheet's journal reports that he was wounded on 24 December 1915 and that he arrived back in England on 22 January 1916.

Grace aged 18 years seated on wall; 1915

An Entry of Marriage, dated 13 June 1916, from Bakewell Register Office reveals the following information:

"Cheetham William Fletcher, Aged 22 years, Bachelor of Hill Head, Bradwell married Grace Pember Bough, Aged 19 years, Spinster of Hill Head, Bradwell". Cheet's occupation is shown as "Private in 3rd Sherwood Foresters (Joiner and Wheelwright)" and Grace's as "Mill Hand" with the inference that she was working, or had worked, at Bamford Mill. Cheet's father John is shown as "Joiner and Wheelwright (Master)" and Grace's father, William Bough (deceased) as "Stonemason (Journeyman)". In attendance were Clarence Hunstone, Registrar, Alf Hawes, Superintendent Registrar and witnesses Frances Middleton and R Atkinson. Cheet's journal states that he was back in France on 15 June 1916 - just two days after his marriage service! An embroidered card to his mother with the message "Hope and Love" was received in October 1916:

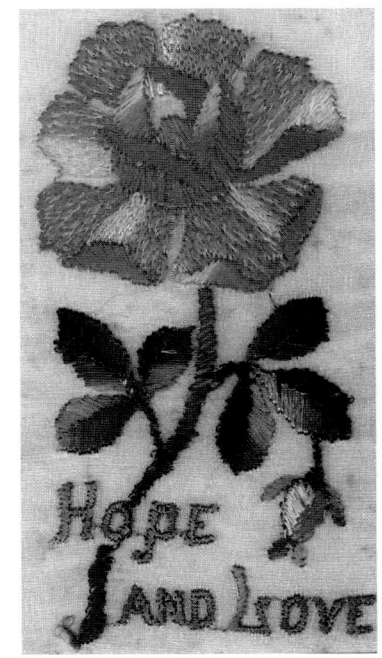

Oct 3rd/1916 To My Dear
Mother from your loving Son
Cheet XXXXX
Remember me to all & Keep
Smiling
Good Luck & Are We
Downhearted
NO XXX

Embroidered card to Annie

In the following year Annie received a green envelope headed "On Active Service", postmarked "Field Post Office, 22 March 1917" and addressed to "Mrs Fletcher, Briar Cottage, Far Hill, Bradwell, Via Sheffield, Derbyshire, England".

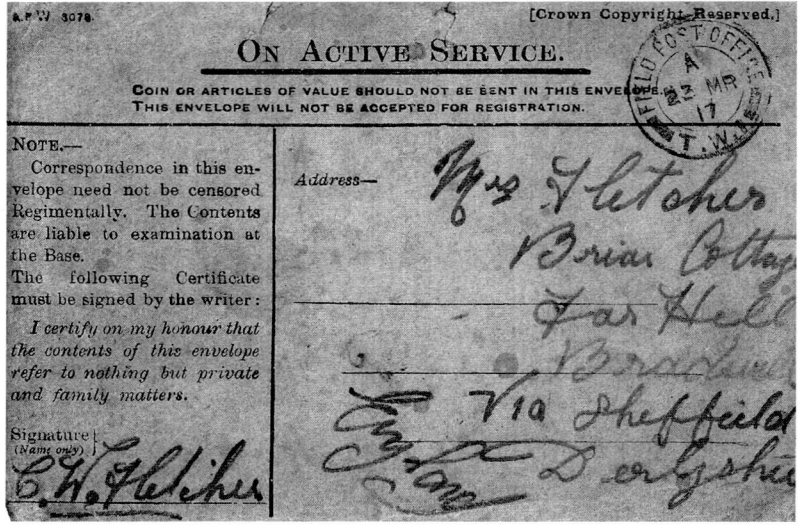

On Active Service Envelope containing letter to Annie

Inside this was a three page letter, written in pencil:

Good Luck   March 22/1917
My Dear Mother X X X X X X X X

Just a few lines in Answer to your ever welcome letter that I have just recieved dated March 16th & I am pleased to hear that you are all in the best of health & spirits as it leaves me as happy as old King Dick at present & in the best of health. You said in your letter that you were thinking of moving into Mrs. Halls house when she moved & that Grace was talking of taking ours on well I am pleased to hear of it, & I shall leave everything entirely in her hands as I have told her

in a good many letters. I shant know what ails me when I can come to a home of my own. My word it will seem grand & thanks for buying us the Table. I thought I would send you the Green Envelope & put Graces inside & then you could see how I was getting on. Well Mother I should like to see you all at home again. It seems a long while since I left you all but I am glad to hear you all are keeping in the Pink. Just Remember me to all & to Grandma. Tell them all I am in the Pink & I don't think it will be very long before its all over. I am sorry to hear of Polly Rowerth. Our Jack is a very lucky lad Mother tell him I say so & also tell him to stick to his job & not loose it & I also think Betty Sykes is a nice Girl I dont know much about the other one he had. Tell him I should like to have a few lines from him & know how he is getting along. We get Plenty to Eat & Drink out here & plenty of good warm clothes so we are alright. My Pals are just having tea it will be cold if I dont go & the Cook will be getting ratty. So will close now.
So just remember me to all.

Wishing you all the best of luck

from your Loving Son Cheet

To my Dear Mother & Father & all

XXXXXX
XXXXX
XXX
X

We aint Downhearted Yet Not Me

In late 1917, Annie Fletcher received a Sherwood Foresters, 139th Infantry Brigade Christmas Card bearing the message "With every good wish for a Happy Christmas" and signed from "Cheetham to Mother".

Front of 139th Infantry Brigade Christmas Card

Picture inside Christmas Card

Onto pages 104-107 (inc) of his journal Cheet' copied his diary for 1918 which he must have recorded during that year whilst he was serving in France. His complete entries are given below:

Diary kept by C W Fletcher 1918.

1918
FEBRUARY

3	In the trenches
4	In the trenches
5	In the trenches Made a raid on Fritze Got some prisoners
6	In the trenches
7	In the trenches We can hear Fritz digging under
8	In the trenches our trench
9	In the trenches We wonder whats going to Happen
10	In the trenches with the Tap tap Tapping
11	In the trenches our artillary shelling heavy
12	In the trenches Trench blown up but I escaped at 11-30 PM
13	In the trenches
14	In the trenches Raided Fritze but we were Repulsed
15	In the trenches Germans Raided us we repulsed them
16	Came back into Supports - 2nd Line of Trenches
17	In Supports
18	In Supports
19	In Supports
20	In Supports
21	Got relieved at 2 AM. NOTE 19 Days in Trenches

22	At Rest behind the Trenches at Ernie St Julian
23	My leave came through
24	Crossed From France to England on 14 Days Leave

MARCH

10	Back in France after the 14 days Leave
11	Arrived at Buivrey
12	Still at Buivrey
13	Went in advance to Trenches in La Bassee Sector
14	In Trenches Got Shelled Heavy lost several Men
15-16	Went Digging Graves in Cambrin Cemetary
17-19	Still in Trenches
20	Relieved from Trenches went to Buvreay for Rest
21	Went back to 465 Coy. Field R.E.s expecting Germans making Gas attack
22-24	Waiting in Trenches but no Gas attack
25-26	Shelling heavy on both sides
27	Relieved & marched to Cite St Perre
28	Marched to Trenches in Levis Sector
28-30	Still in Trenches

APRIL

1	We saw 3 Observation Balloons & 1 plane fetched down by our Airmen
2	Another plane fetched down
3	Fritze Gassed us several of our Chaps Gassed
4	Returned to Cite St Perre in Supports I was on Gas Sentry duty
5	Still at Cite St Perre went for a Bath under Church

6	Back to the Trenches
7	Trenches
8	Came back to Bully court
9	Resting Bully court
10-11	Resting Bully court
12	Moved from Bully to Verquin in Motor Lorries
13-14	Marched from Verquin to Houchin for Rest
15-17	Resting at Houchin
18	Moved from Houchin to Cambrin 4 pals wounded
19-20	In Cambrin Sector
21	Our chaps got 4 pigs from Aniquin Killed & eaten
22	Still in Cambrin
23	Marched from Cambrin to Essars
24-27	In Essars
28	Marched from Essars to Vaudricourt & Heavily Shelled
29-30	March from Vaudricourt to Loisin to Trenches

MAY

1-2	March from Vaudricourt to Loisin to Trenches
3-6	Relieved from Trenches not sorry Awful Trenches
7-10	Came to Liqusnoy in reserve
11	Marched back to Verquin
12-13	Resting at Verquin
14	Back in Trenches got Shelled
15-19	In Trenches Locon Sector, No peace from Shells
20	Moved to Le-Hamel Trenches
21-22	On Tump Line work very dangerous Fritze keeps putting Barrages on us

23-24	Still in Le hamel Sector
25	Relieved and went back for rest at Vaudricourt
26-29	Resting at Vaudricourt, drilling all the Time
30	Battallion moved from Vaudricourt to Lequesnoy
31	In Supports

JUNE

1	Expecting Fritze to Make an attack
2	Still in Supports Standing to, Fritze did not attack
3-11	Resting at Gorre
11	Moved from Gorre to Trenches in Le Hamel Sector
12-16	In Trenches
17	Gas Shelled us very Heavy
18	We make an attack all Objectives obtained Germans lost Heavily
19	Back to Verquin for Rest
20-23	Resting at Verquin we need it bad
24	Went to Bethune
24-30	Resting in Bethune

JULY

1	Back in Trenches in Lehamel
1-14	In Trenches not so Bad
15-21	Resting at Vaudricourt
21-29	Back to Trenches on Supports, Supports worse than Trenches, Heavily Shelled
30	Made Cross for Lt Pearce A Company Killed in Action 22-7-18
31	Relieved & went to Verquin for rest

AUGUST

1 to 7	Resting in Verquin
8	Back to Trenches in Gorre Sector
9	Fritze Gas Shelled us again
10-11	Went with party down to the dump, Cantarra dump Fritze came over in his planes & Bombed the dump & afterwards Shelled us very Heavy
12	Went down to the Sandpits between Lequisnvy & Beuvery
13	Standing to in Sandpit
14	Marched from Sandpit to Essares in Supports
15-16	In Supports
17	Moved up to Lehamel left Sector to Trenches
18	Souter, Garner & Southam my pals got Killed
19	Still in Lehamel Trenches
20	Went to Canal with pontoon Bridge to put across Canal Then came down to Vaudricourt wood
21	In Vaudricourt Wood
22-23	In Vaudricourt Wood Fritze always Shelling
24	Went digging Anti Tank Trap Trenches on left of Gorre wood, 1 Killed 5 Wounded in our party
25	In Vaudricourt wood. Came across A Maltby
26	Went up to Trenches lost several men getting up
27	In Trenches Loisne Sector
28-31	In Trenches Loisne Sector Shelling rather Hot

SEPTEMBER

1	Fritz starts retiring we move over & Take his Trenches

2	In German Trenches
3	8th Sherwood Foresters move and attack but Cannot find Fritz anywhere
4	We moved on after Fritze, nearly got Killed with one of his mines it blew up when about 15 yards off
5	Still moving after Fritz
6	We got relieved & went to Bethune & then to Lapuqnoy
7-10	Resting
11	Entrained Travelled all night & arrived at Corbie
12	on the Somme. Then marched to Lahousossoye
13-22	Resting at Lahousossoye everyone wondering whats up
23	Moved up to Trenches near Fletchin
24	Fritze retiring, keeps putting Barrage on us.
25	George Holmes, another pal got Killed. We make an attack & take over a Hundred prisoners on St Quintin Sector. The prisoners are fed up.
26-29	Fritze makes a faint Counter attack but we easily repulse him, but lose several men
30	We went over the Top again & Gained all Objectives

OCTOBER

1	Went Back for rest at Billinyries
2-3	2nd. Lt. R Lakeman 2nd. Lt. Burrows Killed in Action.
4	Still at Billingries
5-8	Standing to we dont Know whats happening.
9	Moved up to Magney La Fosse
10	Moved to Merricourt
11	Burying Ours & German Dead
12	Germans Still retiring Fast

13	Got to Bohain
14-16	Still in Bohain
17	We go into action & gain all our Objectives
18-31	Easy time in & around Bohain

NOVEMBER

1	We heard that Turkey & Austria had packed in
2	We move up the line to start our offensive
3	We move up to Cantillion the Germans have just left as we move in, All sorts of Traps set.
4	We move through Cantillion, only machine Gun posts to overcome, We lose a few men doing it
5	We get all we go after, Fritze is retiring fast
6	We are after him day & night, We havent any food to eat so order comes Eat your Iron Rations, but thats not enough, we are going so fast they cannot get the Food up to us, Still everyone is Cheerfull Roads etc Blown up by Fritze as he retires Still we keep going Forward
7-8	We get relieved & go back to Petit La Fayt
9	We go up the line & Take Bellinglese Canal the Germans are Surrendering in Hundreds
10	We still go Forward people in some of the Villages have been under the German Rule since 1914 arnt they pleased when they see us, but they have no food to give us the Germans take everything back with them

11   The war is over, We cannot hardly believe it.
*12   We move back to Landrecies, its not far
           from Mons.*
DECEMBER
*16   Our Colour party arrive back from England
           I fix the Kings & Battalion Colours in
           Headquarters Messroom at Landrecies*

*I enlisted Sep 7th 1914 in the Sherwood Foresters
Arrived in France Feb 27th 1915.
Wounded on Dec 24th 1915. Arrived in England Jan 22nd 1916.
Arrived in France again June 15th 1916 until the end of the War.*

On Saturday 5 September, 1914, under the heading "SHEFFIELD RECRUITING - Opening of the Jungle and Corn Exchange", The Sheffield Telegraph reported:

"Any Sheffield young man, physically fit, who wishes to become a soldier and do his duty . . . . can now join the Army in half an hour . . . . At the Jungle, or Corn Exchange, you can go in at one door an ordinary civilian, and out at another a fully attested recruit, having in the meantime been measured, medically examined, sworn in, and received your first day's pay."

A little more light is thrown on the location of the Jungle from the Sheffield Star of Wednesday the first of September, 1948 which commented "The Jungle was the name previously given to the building now occupied by the Townhead Street bus garage which used to be the Winter home of a menagerie. Amongst it's attractions was a performance where a young woman placed her head in a lion's mouth."

We know that the reference in the Derbyshire Courier of 15 January 1916 to Cheet' serving with the Yorks and Lancs regiment is a mistake because he enlisted with the Sherwood Foresters. All known facts authenticate this, including correspondence with Cliff Housley, Regimental Historian, The Sherwood Foresters.

Cheet's daughter-in-law, Joyce Fletcher, remembered being told that Cheet' and Grace had to obtain a special licence for their marriage and also that they had walked from Bradwell to Bakewell to attend the Register Office. Unfortunately there was a misunderstanding about dates which resulted in their presenting themselves one day early. Apparently they had to walk back home and repeat the exercise the following day to become man and wife.

Apart from his detailed diary entries of 1918 little is known of Cheet's whereabouts during the war. Joyce had been told that at some time during WW1 Cheet' was overseeing some German Prisoners of War. She has two brass items, a vase and a whistle made from shell and bullet cases, which she believes were fashioned by German PoWs and given to Cheet'. Items of correspondence have survived but these do not refer to sources because people on active service overseas were not allowed to mention their locations. Cheet' tended to use expressions such as "In France, Somewhere in France and on Active Service".

Cheet's eldest grandson, Barry Fletcher, has five embroidered greetings cards sent to Grace during the war. Their embroidered greetings include "To my dear Bride, To my Dear Wife, Forget Me Not and 1918 A Happy New Year". Inside these cards are smaller card inserts on which Cheet' wrote terms of endearment to his dear wife.

Further undated cards are mentioned below with their embroidered messages and the words written by Cheet':

Souvenir de France, Armes de Jeanne d'Arc:

From your son on Active Service - To My Dear Mother from your Loving Son Cheet
Just Keep Smiling

To my dear Brother:

From France
To My dear Brother Colin From Your loving Brother with best love CW XXXXXX
Dear Colin
Just a line to let you know I am still alive & kicking hoping you are the same. How should you like to come & have a fight with the Germans, it would just suite you I know. Never mind the War will soon be over & I shall be able to come & see you. I thank you for the fags you sent me. Just remember me to our Jack & Stanley & everybody at Bradda. Keep Smiling & dont get down in the Dumps. Eh What. Good Luck Lad & Keep Smiling. C

Keep the house and home:

To My Dear Mother from your Son Cheet
I am still in the Pink
Good Luck
XXXXXX

Embroidered Card to Mother, Annie    *Embroidered Card to brother, Colin*

Embroidered Card to Annie    *Cheet' in dress uniform*

Good Wishes (with card insert and bearing the words Remembrance Souvenir de Glorieuse Memoire):

Mrs Fletcher, Briar Cottage, Bradwell
With best love from Cheetham To Mother & all
XXXXXXXXX   Good Luck

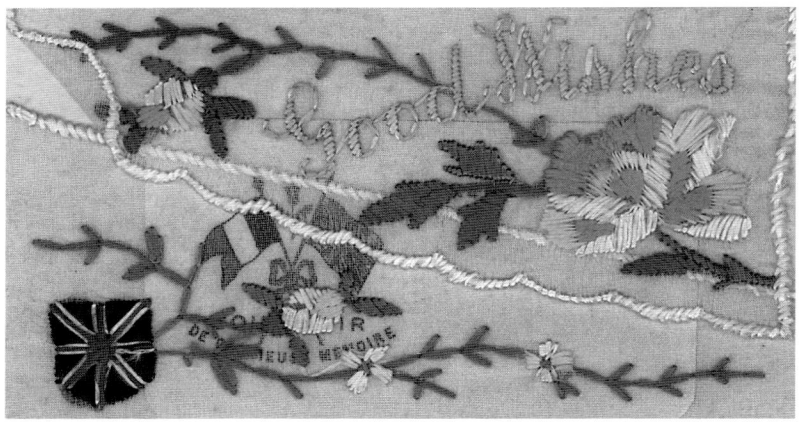

Good Wishes embroidered card to his mother

Cheet's letter dated 22 March 1917 to his mother shows her address as Briar Cottage, Far Hill. There is a reference to his mother (and father) moving to another house which would probably be Hills View, also at Far Hill. Implicitly, Grace would live in Briar Cottage and build this into their first real home in anticipation of Cheet's safe return from France. In the same letter Cheet' mentioned his younger brother Jack, who at that time would be twenty one years of age. Betty Sykes is mentioned and she and Jack went on to become man and wife. Jack had enlisted in the Sherwood Foresters and had been stationed at Cannock Chase. With less than one year's service he had been found to have a heart murmur and he was discharged on medical grounds.

Brother Jack in Sherwood Foresters' Uniform

Grace's brother Harry

Grace, standing right, outside the Bath Hotel where she was in service for a time

Moving on to entries in Cheet's 1918 diary, Cliff Housley, the Regimental Historian of the Sherwood Foresters supplied the following corroborative information relating to casualties:

Arthur Carlton Pearce, Lieutenant, of Hampstead, London, was killed in action on 22 July 1918 when serving in the trenches in the Essars (left Sub-Sector), France. He is buried at Fouquieres Churchyard cemetery, France.

F A Southam, Private, of Ashby De La Zouch, Leicestershire, was killed in action on 18 August 1818 when serving in the trenches near Gorre, France. He is buried at Fouquieres Churchyard extension, France.

Leonard Victor Burrows, 2nd Lieutenant, of Belper, Derbyshire, was killed in action on 1st September 1918 when taking part in the attack on Richebourg, France. He is buried at Fouquieres Churchyard extension, France.

George H Holmes, Sergeant, of Nottingham, was killed in action on 24 September 1918, when in the attack on Beux and Leduc trenches, near Pontruet, France. He has no known grave and is commemorated at the Vis-En-Artois Memorial, France.

Reginald Noel Lakeman, 2nd Lieutenant, of Uxbridge, Middlesex, was killed in action on 3 October 1918 during the attack on, and capture of, the villages of Ramicourt and Montbrehain, France. He is buried at the Bellicourt British cemetery, France.

In his 1918 diary Cheet' mentioned a number of place names. As someone who did not speak French he may have found difficulty in making connections between spoken and written names. From a variety of sources the following list has been compiled to show French place names which most closely match the majority of those found in his journal.

Aniquin	Annequin (E of Bethune)
Bellinglese	Bellenglise (N of St Quentin)
Bethune	Bethune
Beuvery	Beuvry (50 miles SE of Calais)
Billingries	Bellenglise (N of St Quentin)
Billinyries	Bellenglise (N of St Quentin)
Bohain	Bohain (N E of St Quentin)
Buivrey	Beuvry (50 miles S E of Calais)
Buvreay	Beuvry (50 miles S E of Calais)
Bully court	Bellicourt (N of St Quentin)
Cambrin	Cambrin (E of Bethune)
Cite St Perre	Cite St Pierre
Corbie	Corbie (E of Amiens)
Essares	Essars
Essars	Essars
Fletchin	Flechin (N W of St Quentin)
Gorre	Gorre (near Le Hamel)
Houchin	Houchin (S of Bethune)
La Bassee	la Bassee
Landrecies	Landrecies
Lehamel	Le Hamel
Le-Hamel	Le Hamel
Lequesnoy	le Quesnoy (E of Bethune)
Lequisnvy	le Quesnoy (E of Bethune)
Liqusnoy	le Quesnoy
Magney La Fosse	Magny-la-Fosse (N of St Quentin)

Merricourt	Mericourt (S of Lens)
Mons	Mons
Petit La Fayt	(possibly Fayet, N W of St Quentin)
St Quintin Sector	St Quentin (50 miles E of Amien)
Vaudricourt	Vaudricourt (S of Bethune)
Verquin	Verquin (S of Bethune)

In his book "Panorama of the Western Front", John Laffin refers to the town of Bethune, situated to the South West of Ypres in Northern France. "The large town of Bethune was a major forward base and billeting centre for British and Commonwealth troops for much of the war." Regarding St Quentin "the Germans held the city for years and in March 1918 it was one of their main bases for the Spring offensive. The French army, with British help, recaptured the wrecked city on 1st October 1918."

From "A Brief History of the Sherwood Foresters" by English Life Publications, "when World War I (1914-18) was declared the Sherwood Foresters consisted of 8 Battalions and a depot at Derby. During the war the regiment expanded to a maximum of 33 Battalions, of which 20 served overseas. In total 140,000 men, mostly from Nottinghamshire and Derbyshire, served in the regiment.

With the outbreak of war the Territorial Army was immediately mobilised and the original four Sherwood Forester Territorial Battalions combined to form the 139 (Forester) Infantry Brigade in the 46 (North Midland) Division. In February 1915, the 139th (Forester) Brigade had the distinction of being part of the first Territorial Division to land in France. This Brigade served in France for the rest of the war and suffered severe casualties. On the opening day of the Battle of the Somme (1 July 1916) it suffered 80% casualties. The Brigade received special recognition for its magnificent part in the breaking of the Hindenburg Line in the final defeat of the German Army in Autumn 1918."

The Regiment's War Memorial at Crich, in the form of a lighthouse tower, was dedicated in 1923 in memory of the 11,409 men of the Sherwood Foresters who gave their lives in the 1914-18 war.

In Bradwell Churchyard is to be found the War Memorial which lists "The men of this parish who fell in the Great War". Listed amongst the 33 casualties is the name L E A Middleton who could have been the young Lionel Middleton who enlisted with Cheet' and Percy Bradwell on 7 September 1914. Also listed is A Maltby, almost certainly Arthur Maltby, referred to in Chapter One as a member of the village 'gang' and the same person that Cheet' met in Vaudricourt Wood on 25 August 1918.

Taken from a supplement to The London Gazette of Tuesday 8 July, 1919 headed War Office, 9 July, 1919:

"The following is a continuation of Sir D Haig's despatch of 16 March, 1919, submitting names deserving of Special Mention:-" Within the body of the document and under the heading of "Nottinghamshire & Derbyshire Regiment", a one line entry:

"Fletcher, 203491 L./C. (A./Sjt.) C. W., 1/5th Bn. (T.F.)"

Cheet's youngest grandson, William Cheetham Fletcher is guardian of three medals awarded to his grandfather during the First World War. These are a circular Victory Medal, a First World War Star and a circular British War Medal.

The War of 1914-1918.

Nottinghamshire & Derbyshire Regt.
203491 L./C. (A./Sjt.) C. W. Fletcher, 1/5th Bn. (I.F.)

was mentioned in a Despatch from
Field Marshal Sir Douglas Haig, K.T. G.C.B. O.M. G.C.V.O. K.C.I.E.
dated 16th March 1919
for gallant and distinguished services in the Field.
I have it in command from the King to record His Majesty's
high appreciation of the services rendered.

Winston S. Churchill
Secretary of State for War.

War Office
Whitehall S.W.
1st July 1919.

Mentioned in Despatches Certificate

In his journal Cheet' produced two other pieces of writing which relate to the period 1914-18 and these are included here for completeness. Referring to late 1914 or early 1915, which was the period of his basic training in the North East of England, he wrote the following short story:

A True Ghost Story by C W Fletcher:

Early in the 1914-1919 War:

I was on Sentry one night from 12 am until 2 am in front of the Esplanade Hotel, at Whitley Bay. Everything was very quiet, not a sound to be heard except the sea. I was taking things easy when all at once I thought I heard a noise, so I listened. Then I heard pitter, patter, pitter, patter. It sounded like some kind of an animal. I listened again; pitter, patter, pitter, patter, then all at once I saw something white coming towards me.

So I shouted Halt, who goes there? I got no answer. Then I shouted again, still no response, this white thing getting nearer and nearer. So I lifted my rifle up and released the bolt, which of course made a noise. Then I heard someone say, don't shoot Sentry, don't shoot. And there it was, one of our Officers, who had been to Tynemouth to a dance, and with him he had one of the Maids, from the Waverley Hotel, and they had got their dancing Slippers on and the Young Lady had a White dress on.

Anyway I told them they were lucky I hadn't fired at the White dress, as I thought at first it was a Ghost. The Officer popped me half a crown in my hand and told me not to report it and you bet I didn't. I think they were lucky. If it had been a nervous Sentry he would have shot after the first Challenge.

Cheet' also wrote the following poem to which he gave the title "A Brave Lad". Whether or not the events in the poem are taken from his personal experience we will never know.

A Brave Lad, as seen by C W Fletcher

'Twas on the Battle Field of Belgium
A Wounded Soldier Lay
This Soldier's Name's not Mentioned
It would not do to say.
You might say that you Knew Him
It might be an only Son
The night was cold & very dim
And Snow lay on his Gun
His Head lay on his Arm, poor lad
His Legs he could not Move
That Lad he cried & Sighed, Ho dad
Your Son you're going to lose
I held him up within my Arms
And Gave The Lad a drink
I dressed his wounds then he was calm
So he said just let me think
That Lad was Brave until the Last
The Pain he Bravely Bore
A Lad he was just Seventeen past
He never Turned a Hair
He said dear pal a line just Write
to let my Mother Know

Her Son did die for right gainst Might
But do not Blame the Foe
And just tell them to forgive me
For running away from Home
I thought it best it would be
As I did like to Roam
Tell them I'm one of Many
Who died for Home and King
And give my love to Fanny
The Girl I gave the ring
My Girl I Know she will be Sad
And I Know she'll Cry
But tell her not to take it Bad
As We've all got to die
That Lad he passed away in Peace
When he had told me all
And then his head I did release
To Gently let it Fall
I saw him Buried in a Grave
A Blanket for a Shroud
I thought it hard for one so Brave
And one so very proud

Diary kept by C. W. Fletcher 1918.

Nov	2	We move up the line to start our offensive
"	3	We move up to Cantillon. The Germans have just left as we move in. All sorts of Traps set.
	4	We move through Cantillon, only machine gun posts to overcome. We loose a few men doing it.
	5	We get all we go after, Fritze is retiring fast
	6	We are after him day & night. We havnt any food to eat so order comes Eat your Iron Rations, but thats not enough, we are going so fast they cannot get the Food up to us, still everyone is cheerfull. Roads etc Blown up by Fritze as he retires. Still we keep going Forward.
7 & 8	8	We get relieved & go back to Petit La Fayet
	9	We go up the line & take Bellinglese Canal the Germans are Surrendering in Hundreds
-	10	We still go Forward people in some of the Villages have been under the German Rule since 1914 arnt they pleased when they see us, but they have no food to give us the Germans take everything back with them
Nov.	11	The war is over, We cannot hardly believe it.
"	12	We move back to Landrecies, its not far from Mons.
Dec	16	Our Colour party arrive back from England I fix the Kings & Battalion Colours in Headquarters Messroom. at Landrecies

Page 107 of Cheet's journal

Chapter 3
Between The Wars

One day we were working at Mrs Joe Bramall's when she lived near the Bethlehem Chapel. Myself and Ted Knowles were pulling an old porch down just outside the front door. We found part of an old purse, so I put my hand in my pocket, and wrapped about 15/- in the old purse, then we buried it in the garden near the porch. When Mrs Bramall came out, of course we found the old purse with the money in. What have you found she says, so we opened the purse and shared the money between myself, and Ted. When we came back from our Dinners, There was Mrs Bramall, Mrs Albert Bradwell, and Mrs Walton, poking with Sticks and poker, expecting to find more money. We had to Laugh.

I was working in Hugh Lane where Miss Wragg lives repairing the Stairs. I had to go underneath the Stairs to fix a prop. One of George Haywards Grandsons was watching me at the time. As I was working I found a rat hole and in the rat hole was an old Mustard Tin wrapped with cloth that had been dipped in Tar. I took the lid off and put about 10/- worth of silver in the Tin, the Boy not seeing me do it. When the Boy saw me pull the tin out of the Hole and open it and the money inside his eyes nearly popped out of his head. Of course the lad ran out and told his Grandad what I had found. He came round to see if it was true, so I said yes, but I didn't tell him how much was in the tin. Well I went home to Tea, when I came back there was Mr and Mrs Hayward under the Stairs with a candle each looking if there was any more money to be found. It got round Bradwell that I had found a Tin full of

Sovereigns. Miss Wragg came to see me thinking it was True, until I told her it was only a Joke. To this day I think that Miss Wragg thinks I found a Tin full of Money under the Stairs.

Myself and Ted Knowles were working at a house one day, and the Woman was ever so busy Cleaning. All at once Ted said to the Woman, I should have thought you would have been at the Tea, instead of Cleaning. What Tea says the woman. Why said Ted haven't you heard, the Co-operative people are giving a free Tea, and a Free parcel to each of their Members. I've never heard anything about it and I am a Member. Anyway about half an hour later out comes the Woman in her Sunday best and she went to the Memorial Hall expecting a free Tea and parcel. Didn't she swear when she came back. What a Joke.

A TRUE GHOST STORY AS SEEN BY MY SELF -
C W Fletcher:

It was at the time I was living at Hall Barn or Old Barn as it is mostly called. One night, myself, wife and two friends were having a game of cards. We had been playing for a couple of hours or more. Anyway it would be about one o'clock in the morning. Everything as quiet as the Dead, when suddenly: THUD, THUD, THUD.

What's that says my Friend. I don't know I said, It's perhaps one of the Children upstairs, I'll pop up and look. No it wasn't that as the children were sleeping Soundly. Anyway, we started to play cards again, when all at once the THUD, THUD, THUD started again.

I had a big Black dog at the time which Started to Growl. These Friends of mine had come over from Sheffield, so his Wife says Ho it's a Ghost. Well to tell you the Truth I began to think so. Well I had been upstairs so I thought I would have a look in the other rooms which I did but could not find anything. So I sat down again, all at once THUD, THUD, THUD, again for ever so many times. The dog growled again, everybody went white. So I got the dog on the Lead and went to the back door and into the back Yard. No I couldn't hear anything there so I came back into the house again and sat down.

We didn't feel inclined to play cards again, so we sat listening. A few minutes after, THUD, THUD, THUD, again. Well, I didn't like it I'll tell you, so I put the dog's lead on. Well if you Notice the Window facing in Greaves's Croft it's nearly level to the Field. When I had got the dog on the Lead I went through the Front door and on the lane a bit and I Listened in the dark and do you know what it was that was making the Thudding noise? Why an old horse which was close to the window, and I think it's Foot must have been Itching and it made it paw the ground with it's foot.

Wasn't myself, and the others Thankful when I had found it out. If I hadn't found it I should have Thought someone's Ghost was prowling around Hall Barn.

Hall Barn or Old Barn is situated on Jeffrey Lane, Bradwell and Cheet' and Grace are believed to have lived there for a time.

A TRUE TALE by C W Fletcher

Myself and Ted Knowles were working at Mrs Rachel Hall's house up Far Hill. I was Varnishing the front door and Ted Knowles was painting the Front Window. Mrs Rachel Hall was knitting a pair of Socks near the Fire. As myself and Ted were talking Mrs Hall kept joining in the Conversation.

All at once Ted says to me, lets see, what time does the Elephant come to Bradwell. So I knew in a moment it was a joke. Well I said, they say the Elephant comes to the Town Bottom at 2.30. Yes says Ted and the Elephant wears a Waistcoat and tells you the time with a Watch it's got in it's Waistcoat pocket. I said yes and it dances on an apple barrel, {now you just fancy an Elephant on an Apple Barrel}.

What's that says Rachel. So we told her again, adding more to it. Ha says Rachel, Ha mon goo un tell arr Ann, so off she went. Well do you know, the people up Far Hill and Hill Head kept their children away from School and went down to see the Elephant which wasn't there, & Mrs Hall and her Sister dressed up in their Sunday Best.

I won't tell you what they said when they came back. It ought to have been the first of April.

A TRUE TALE

I was talking to a man one day, his name is Millingham, he lives near the steps on the Hills. He was telling me he had never had a Headache, or anything whatever the matter with him in his life. A few weeks after I saw him again. My word he said, the other night about Midnight I was took bad with pains in my Stomach. I felt so Bad I thought I was dying, so I sent the Wife for the Doctor. When he had examined me he said, you're alright it's only a touch of Stomach ache you've got. What is it you've been eating. He said he never felt such a Fool in his life, calling the Doctor in for Stomach ache, and I bet he didn't.

A TRUE TALE

Allan Elliott used to dig the Graves in the Primitive Chapel Yard. He worked at Bamford Mill and had the Gravedigging job as a spare time Job. He got up early one morning and he was in the Grave (and it wasn't daylight) shovelling away, when all at once something white loomed above him. What art Thou doing says the thing in White. I believe Allan jumped out of the Grave and ran Home. The Lady in white was old Mary Philip in her nightdress having a walk out. Allan said he would never dig another Grave and he hasn't done up to now. It nearly scared him stiff. He was ill for weeks after. Poor old Allan.

TALES OF THE WHITE HART by C W FLETCHER:

> In Towngate Bradwell stands a pub
> White Hart's its Bonny name
> You get a drink, Straight from the Tub
> Its noted for its Fame
> This pub was built in 16 Something

The Landlord's Name's Jim Knowles
He brings a drink thats fit for Kings
It goes down to your soles
They play their game of dominoes
And some good players they've got
they Shuffle, draw, to find who's Foes
And then the game gets Hot
Old Shirley looks at Marking Board
To see what Cooper's doing
And old Bill's voice its like a Lord
When Shirley's just Cheating
There's Fletcher, Dan and Williams too
They say they're very Keen
Stan & Jack & Hernshaw too
are very often Seen
Old Bill, he likes his pints Galore
Shirley he cannot Stand
He says that Shirley makes him Sore
He Holds them in his Hand
Now Shirley likes his pocket full
of Bacca and of Fags
and when he's looking very dull
you bet his pocket sags
Fred Senior likes a Game as well
His play I like to see
Another thing you ne'er can tell
what Fred has on his Knee

I went one night to have a drink
Old Bill was in a Stew
He said that Shirley had a Kink
The dominoes were New
He said that Shirley had them Marked
I think his words were True
for Shirley when he gets his seat
is fixed the whole night through
There's Albert Quince he likes a Quart
Also his pipe of Twist
Bill Williams Sits like Sir James Stewart
With Glass tight in his Fist
From on Townend up comes our Jim
His Medicine he likes
A nice chap Jim we all like Him
Although he never Bikes
Now Horace likes his Magnet Bright
He Smacks his lips with pride
He comes & goes times every Night
I think he must be Hired
There's Kelly Dabber others too
Their names I cannot think
And if they are not mentioned, do
Please not cause a Stink
I saw a Bit on Christmas Eve
they say He lives up Lane
He Visits Jim just Christmas Eve

And brings his voice & cane
You see, that Night Jim Gives Free Beer
Sandwiches & Mince Pies
They say he stuffed and very near
Drank poor Jimmy dry
At Holiday time you see our Mac'
That Scotsman's heart is True
And Felix, Ted they have their Snack
And Drink old Jimmies Brew

James Henry Knowles was landlord of the White Hart in the 1930s. Old Shirley refers to Shirley Swindels who lived at the bottom of 'The Stones' in the house accessed by steps. Fletcher, line 17, probably refers to Cheet's father, John Fletcher and Dan could be Dan Middleton. Jim, line 45, most likely refers to Jim Wilson, father of Ben, David and John. Horace, line 49, probably refers to Horace Eyre who lived in Stretfield. McGibbons was probably a future landlord of the White Hart (source Wilf Cushworth).

Of further interest, Brian and Pam Fletcher (Cheet's nephew and his wife) ran the White Hart from 1980 to 1984.

A FEW LINES ABOUT SOME BRADDA LADS WHO WENT CAROL SINGING:

Twa's Christmas, Nineteen Thirty nine
Six Lads came to our door
They Guised themselves and did look fine
Their Singing it was poor.

Now George was like a parson old
and Tommy's eyes were glazed
Wilfred Ho, he looked so Bold
poor Bill he was quite dazed.

Roy & Noel weren't so Bad
they hadn't much to drink
poor Wilfred who did look so sad
kept giving poor Eve the Wink.

They went to Williams, drank some Ale
And Gave them Christmas songs
Tom drank that Ale, just like a Whale
and said he'd never done Wrong.

Next door at Fletcher's, they had some port
As smoke reeked from their Fags
poor Billy said, ho, what a fort
lets stop and rest our legs.

Three Girls were with those Boys that night
And two had drank enough
Both Gene and Eve looked in a plight
But Nance, she doesn't puff.

*At last they went to Sailor Sam's
And Sailor poured it neat
I think those lads, they wanted Trams
For Home, or England's Fleet.*

*When Sailor's whiskey was quite done
they went on Rhubarb Wine
With faces like the Rising Sun
They couldn't walk the line.*

*Eve and Gene said just one More
before you all go Home
A Tot of Rum, we will just pour
before you go to Roam.*

*So Bill said well we'll just have one
to wish you all the best
Tom said well I'll be a Mon
before I go to Rest.*

*So off they went to take Bill Home
It took them all an Hour
And Bill upstairs did quietly roam
With Stomach very Sour*

Then off the others, up to Hill Head
But they kept falling down
I heard that Wilf was sick in Bed
And Tom lay in the Town.

Poor Roy was Fagged when he got back
And stopped in bed next day
Although he didn't have his wack
He said it did not pay.

They sang, while Shepherds watch, three times
Poor Gene, she did not know
She said she did not care for chimes
Lets have run Bunny, slow.

Eve had the Box of Money
She Clung to it like Honey
My word her eyes they did look Funny
When Gene had mentioned Bunny.

When Wilfred landed home next Morn
he left the Gas Full on
He spilled the milk at nearly dawn
Then he was fairly gone.

Strictly speaking this poem was set after the outbreak of WW2 - however it has been included in this chapter because it comes across as pure Bradwell social life and makes no reference whatsoever to the war. The six lads, in order of appearance, were George Fletcher (Cheet's nephew), Tommy Hartle, Wilfred Cushworth, Bill Cooper, Roy Fletcher (Cheet's son) and Noel Fletcher (Cheet's nephew).

Seven young men enjoying a Sunday walk to the Gliding Club at Great Hucklow (circa 1938). Back Row, left to right: Bill Cooper, Wilf Cushworth, Donald Dakin and Clifford Andrew. Front Row: Roy Fletcher, Tommy Hartle and Albert Ashmore.

Wilf Cushworth suggested that the Eve in verse 3 is likely to have been Eva Middleton, the daughter of (Sailor) Sam and Vinny Middleton. Williams in verse 4 probably refers to George Williams who lived in the cottage at Townend which is now named Cheetham Cottage. Gene in verse 6 could refer to Jean Wilson who lived at the top of Micklow.

WHEN SOME BRADDA MEN & WOMEN WENT TO LONDON IN 1939

One day some chaps, to London went
From Bradda moor Bart Hats
They went, & came back bout a cent
Folk said, that they wore spats

Now Bill, who'd never seen a Ship   (Bill Simpson
And thought, the Thames, the Sea   from top of
A night, in London, Bill did Kip   Smalldale)
In Bed, he had some Tea

Now Jim, a night suit, did not take   (Jim Fletcher
A thing, he'd never worn   from Moorbrook)
And when, the Maid to Bed brought cake
Jim wished, he'd never been Born

A Guide was found, who took them round
To have, a look round Town
Twas said, the Guide, did laugh so sound
That he had, to lay him down

Marshall went, in such high Glee   (Little Marshall
And went, to rest at night   Elliott from
He said, that everything was Free   Smalldale)
And drank till he was tight

Miss Needham went, she lost her stick   (Miss
Was lost without that friend   Needham from
She thought, someone, had played a trick   Smalldale
Her temper did not mend   Hall)

Jim went into, a large Hotel
And called, for a pint of best
The Barmaid said, we do not sell
our beer in pints, But less

Jim said, bring me the old pint pot
A glass, I do not like
I like my drink, & like a lot
They do not, call me Mike

Bill Simpson said, by Gum twas great
That trip to London Town
A long time. I shall have to wait
Again to don my Brown

In February 1920, Cheet's maternal grandmother Sarah Hallam died aged 72 years. The grave of Sarah and her husband Cheetham Hallam is situated in the cemetery of Bradwell Methodist Church, Towngate.

On 26 November 1920 Roy Fletcher was born; he was to be the only child of Cheet' and Grace. It seems likely that he was born at Mountain View cottage which is at Far Hill, only a few paces from Rock Hill cottage where Cheetham was born.

A picture postcard of a Bungalow Holiday Home, Penmaenmawr, North Wales, from Grace to Mr C Fletcher, Mountain View, Bradwell, postmarked 13 May 1928 (stamped 1 penny) went on to say:

"Dear Cheet. This is where we are staying the weather is grand & we are having a good time. We landed here half past five it was a bit cold but fine. We have a lot of young girls here full of fun so we are all right. We go to bed at ten but we dont go to sleep theres too much talking and laughing. We are no where near Harrys & Billy his a lot better. I bet Roy as had somethink to say. We are all getting ready for Church (Laugh)
With love Grace X X X X."

The grave of Annie Fletcher's parents; Bradwell Methodist Church

Noel Fletcher, Cheet's nephew, recalled that John Fletcher's original business included cart-making but he had no turning machinery at Bradwell. John used to send Cheet' and Jack on foot to Peak Forest with the heavy blanks of wood to have them turned into wheel hubs at his father's wheelwrighting workshop. Noel confirmed that the Butts workshop was water powered and that the business was based there until 1926/28 before being transferred to Townend.

Colin and Amy - early days

Jack and Betty - early days

Townend joiners' shop

Cheet' taking a short breather from work; July 1924

Grandpa Fletcher with Grandson Roy; July 1924

Cheet's uncle Bill at work in the wheelwrights' workshop, Peak Forest

Noel also remembered his great grandmother Sarah Ann, whose maiden name was Ashton, who used to come and stay in Bradwell for several weeks at a time. May Fletcher recalled a tale she had heard from her husband Jack about how he used to sneak his school pals into the house to see his great grandma smoking her pipe. She was poorly sighted and would ask him if there was any other person in the room. On being told no she would ask Jack to help her fill and light her pipe, much to the amusement of his school friends who no doubt had plenty to talk about when they returned to school.

Noel spoke of the family of his grandmother Annie. She had a sister Polly who married a man named Len Evans. She also had brothers Alf, Ben, Jason (not sure) and Bob. Noel's great uncle Bob was a generous man and he kept a big pot bubbling on his fire from which he fed local poor children. This would have been around 1930 when Noel was six or seven. Some years later Grace would tell her daughter-in-law Joyce of Cheet's uncle Bob coming to visit them. His bulk did not lend itself to low chairs and he dropped himself into a Windsor-type wooden chair, his ample seat covering the sleeping cat's head. The cat's legs were kicking vigorously from beneath him and with all speed Grace somehow bundled Bob off the chair. Because of his kind disposition Bob was most distraught and although the cat was saved, for the rest of its life it could only manage a strangled miaow.

In the 1940s Cheet's uncle Bob was to tell Joyce of the time that he had woken one morning to find his legs in the air, pointing towards the ceiling His head ached and he said to himself "if this is heaven I'm not struck on it". The bed's legs had gone through the floor and Cheet' and Jack had to go and repair the floor. A final story about uncle Bob was that he once fell in the Town and because of his bulk several people were required to get him back onto his feet.

Cheet's grandmother, Sarah Ann Fletcher of Dam Dale Farm, Peak Forest

Joyce Fletcher retold a story that Jack and Cheet' once made a snow sledge and trailer to be able to give lots of children sleigh rides in the snow. Roy and George once took the sled and came speeding down the Town. PC Applegate signalled them to stop (a hopeless request) and he was scooped up by the sled as it raced into Town bottom before crashing into the brook railings and coming to rest. The two lads ran off and the story goes that the sledge was never seen again.

From his home at Mountain View, George Parritt, born 1909, recounted a number of memories of Cheet' and family. Cheet' was shot through the throat in WW1 and also had a bad chest; George wondered if it was from being gassed in the trenches. Cheet' and Jack worked extensively together. In 1933 George was courting his wife to be, Elsie Winkley, who lived at Fern Bank. Grace, Cheet' and Roy lived at Mountain View and around Christmas time Roy had called on George to say that Cheet' would like a word with him.

Roy and grandpa John outside Hills View cottage; circa 1930

Cheet', Grace, Roy & Lil outside Hills View; circa 1931

Seemingly, Cheet' had spoken to his own father John for permission to let George Parritt and his intended take over the rent on the cottage if they so wished. Cheet' and Grace had bought the house at Townend. George was delighted and agreed to take over the rental. Cheet' and Jack redecorated the house from top to bottom and George and Elsie, who had married on the tenth of February 1934, moved in at a weekly rent of four shillings and sixpence. George recalled enquiring about the name of the cottage to which Cheet' had replied that he had always called it 'Mountain View'.

George was offered the cottage, some time later, at a purchase price of £100 but he could not afford it. His rent of 4/6d continued for many years without increase. It was to be more than twenty years after moving in that Grace would come to see him one Sunday night and they would agree a purchase price of £290.

In addition to Mountain View, John Fletcher owned a house at Dialstones for which he received rent from his son Jack who had married Betty Sykes. John and Annie lived at Hills View and he also owned Briar Cottage at Far Hill for which he received rent from Ernest and Cissy Dungworth who were great friends with Cheet' and Grace.

Cissy and Ernest Dungworth outside Briar Cottage

In the event of his death John's will stated that Annie was to receive rents from the four cottages during her lifetime. On her death Hills View was to go to Colin, Mountain View to Cheet' and the Dialstones cottage to Jack. Briar Cottage would be sold and the proceeds shared between the three sons.

Drawing of Townend shop around the time Cheet' and Grace moved in; circa 1934. The right hand cottage in the background is Cheetham cottage. (Reproduced with the permission of Miss H.E. Fischer).

Wilf Cushworth, born in 1921 in Manchester, came to live at Hill Head, Bradwell at the age of four. Wilf, Roy Fletcher and Tommy Hartle were big mates and they attended Bradwell Church school together. Wilf remembered a time when himself, George Fletcher and some others were tormenting John Fletcher, Cheet's father, up near his farm buildings at Hill Head. All at once John chased after them and they scattered in all directions, some of them running down The Town. The old guy chased them and managed to catch George, who was fairly heavy and not a good runner. He pulled George's trousers down and proceeded to give his grandson a thrashing with his leather belt. This confirmed his reputation for being very strict.

A smiling John Fletcher on his small farm

John Fletcher had 4 cows and a horse named Kitty. Wilf, Noel Fletcher and John Fletcher once went to fetch a cow from Peak Forest. All three of them rode on Kitty the horse and Wilf remembered that he fell under the horse as they were going along Green Lane just off the top of Haddleton. Wilf told how they collected the cow in Peak Forest and how he and Noel realised why John had asked them along because on the return journey they spent most of their time herding and guiding the cow whilst John rode all the way back.

John Fletcher shooting. Bradwell Edge can be seen in the background.

Wilf recalled, "Cheet' used to torment us as teenagers. We used to play billiards at Townend and Len Evans, Polly's husband, would join us at weekends and sometimes in the week if we could make the time. Also, we used to play cards for matches - never, ever for money, but of course we would have to buy a box of matches from Cheet' and Grace's shop! I was always made welcome and usually we had coffee and biscuits. I used to call when I went to the 'pictures' which were next door at the Memorial Hall on Tuesdays and Thursdays." Wilf and Dorothy still have a rectangular plate which Cheet' and Grace gave to them as a wedding present and they still use it from time to time.

Grace outside Townend shop; circa 1936

From his home at Mytham Bridge, Bamford, Jack Bough was able to recall some of his memories of Cheet'. He remembered that Cheet' used to head the funeral cortege through Bradwell village and that he would give Jack a wink and a smile as he drew level with him: an example of Cheet's way of dealing with serious business.

Jack told of Cheet' spreading a rumour that the circus was coming to Bradwell with elephants and clowns and that the school children were given the afternoon off.

He also referred to Cheet's walk; apparently a bouncing, springy action because he walked on his toes. He confirmed that Cheet' and Grace owned a motor bike and sidecar and Cheet' wore his cap back-to-front whilst driving it

Cheet' & Grace, taken at Monsal Head, Derbyshire; 15 June 1929

During WW1 Grace's brother Harry had served in the Royal Navy and after the war, with work being very scarce in the Hope Valley, he moved to Wales in search of employment. There he was to meet his future wife, Emily Amelia Broom, set up home and raise a family of 4 children, William, Jack, Celia Maude (Cissy) and Ronald (more often called Roy).

Jack recalled that his Aunt Grace, Jack Fletcher, his Uncle Billy and Aunt Rhoda came to visit them in 1934 in Merthyr Tydfil. Grace and Jack travelled in a motor bike and sidecar, Billy and Rhoda on a motorcycle.

At the time Jack was nine and he mentioned that his father had been out of work for about 18 months which forced the family to "live on the parish". Emily received 31/3d from the parish which was divided into 13/- rent, 17/- to meet all bills and living expenses with Harry receiving the 1/3d. Jack remembered that at this time, aged 9, he would help out at Arnold's the joiners and wheelwrights in Harris Place, Myrthr, in return for which he would receive sixpence a week. This he would use to buy ends of meat from the butchers which would provide for Sunday dinner.

There were times when he did not receive his sixpence until after the butcher had closed in which case some alternative meal had to be found.

During the visit by the Derbyshire foursome it must have been evident that Harry, Emily and family were poorly off and Grace and Billy said they would do all they could to find brother Harry a job back in the Hope Valley. This came to be and Harry started a job at Earl's Cement Works. Initially he came by himself and lived with Cheet' and Grace at Townend whilst he searched for a home for his family. He found an unfurnished cottage to rent near Walker's shop at Town Bottom and started to make arrangements for his family to join him.

Jack Bough was able to recall that "The Parish moved us by train to Sheffield and Uncle Billy met us at the station in his Tram Driver's uniform and took Mother and the four of us to Woolworths for lunch." Their furniture and possessions, following on by rail freight, were misplaced and the family had no alternative but to stay with Cheet' and Grace at Townend until their chattels were found. Eventually their belongings arrived, having taken four weeks to journey from Merthyr Tydfil, and Jack described his aunt Grace throwing her arms in the air and exclaiming "thank God it's arrived!"

Another memory of Jack's was that Cheet' had spread a rumour that Bill and Jack Bough were boxers. Challenges soon came from Bradwell lads and these took a lot of living up to. On one occasion Roy Fletcher challenged Bill Bough to a fight but he wouldn't take him on because Harry had told him not to get involved in fights.

Jack went on to say that they lived at Town Bottom for another four years. On one occasion Harry was off work with an injury and he helped Cheet' with some work on the roof of the cottage at Townend, now known as Cheetham Cottage.

Grace and Cheet' out for a stroll

Roy on holiday in Blackpool; circa 1938

Colin with his second wife, Alice

Cheet' & Grace on garden seat - taken on holiday in Blackpool; circa 1938

Around 1938 Harry started work with Baillie's the Scottish contracting firm, initially labouring and then, after an accident, storekeeping on the Ladybower Reservoir project. Jack's brother Bill worked on the Ladybower reservoir project for a year or so as a winch driver. The family went to live in number 3, Parsons Gate at Yorkshire Bridge. These homes were to be for employees of the water company but were used as temporary accommodation for construction workers during the building of the reservoir.

Jack left school aged 14 and worked as a shop assistant at Hancock's shop in Bamford with a weekly wage of 10/7d. He used to cycle to Bradwell and visit his aunt Grace, sometimes going on to Bradwell pictures at the Memorial Hall.

Bill Bough, Jack's brother confirmed that Emily was living with her parents on Tram Road, Hirwaun, when Harry first met her. After they were married they moved to Myrthr Road, Hirwaun where Bill was born in 1921. Jack and Celia Maude (Cissy) were born at Troedyrhiw, near Aberfan, at 7 Diana Street. Young Brother Roy was born at the family's next home at Harris Place, Merthyr Tydfil. Like his brother Jack, Bill also contributed to the purchase of meat for Sunday lunch by selling bundles of kindling sticks for one old penny.

Once, on his way to school he was faced with a moral dilemma as he was taking a short-cut through Merthyr station. Some boxes of fish were being unloaded and one of the boxes was damaged. He quickly took a fish and concealed it under his clothing, his first thought being that his mother loved fish. He rushed home and presented the fish to Emily who took it, but most reluctantly because she knew it had been stolen. Bill then ran to school, some one and a half miles, where he arrived considerably late. Having been interrogated about his lateness and not having a plausible reason Bill was punished by caning on both hands. He still remembered the details of the incident and the range of good and bad feelings it had provoked.

Bill confirmed that he and Jack used to go to the ex-servicemen's club in Myrthyr and, although they did a bit of boxing, they were certainly not as accomplished as Cheet' had made them out to be with the Bradwell lads.

He spoke of a number of instances where the Bradda lads had made things difficult for him and his brother Jack. He described some of the big differences he experienced in moving from Wales to Bradwell - many of these hinged around language and the new words he had to become accustomed to. Examples he gave included ashmen, bosh, roshins and touch which in Bradwell translated to dustmen, sink, spice and tiggy! A mate or pal in Bradda was a 'butty' in Wales, whereas a brother was pronounced 'brow'. There was also a marked contrast between Bradwell 'hills' which were on a much lesser scale than Welsh 'mountains'.

He remembered coming to Sheffield and being met by his uncle Billy, Grace's brother, who took them to lunch at Woolworths. They were then shown onto the Hope Valley train which took them to Hope station from where Bill Pashley's bus took them to Townend, Bradwell. His face showed fond memories of visiting Bradwell pictures on Tuesdays and Thursdays. He recalled Harry Howe as caretaker, Mr Brown as projectionist and Mrs Brown on the door collecting money. Eva Middleton's mother would sometimes collect the money. One particular night Bill had been tormented relentlessly by George Fletcher. Having warned him a number of times without success Bill struck out and hit George in the face. Harry Howe was going to throw Bill out but Mrs Middleton had seen the whole escapade and was able to smooth the situation. Bill remembered with sadness that that was the last time he saw George who was tragically killed during WW2. Bill often remembered this, his last meeting with George Fletcher.

Bill used to deliver groceries for Wilf Walker and he described their Bradwell address as Walker's yard. From Bradwell they moved to

Yorkshire Bridge and later to Winhill View, Hope Road, Bamford.

He recalled that his grandfather William Bough, Grace's father, had lived at Derwent village which was destroyed by the building of the Ladybower Dam. Prior to the filling of the dam, burial remains were removed from Derwent church to Bamford church where they were commemorated by plain black crosses. He told of a trip that Harry had made to Bamford church to find his parents' grave which on being unsuccessful had led to him calling in at the Derwent Arms. In the bar he had met an old friend who commiserated and imbibed with Harry until some few hours later they parted. Harry set off to ride home on his bicycle and having passed Bamford station proceeded down to Mytham Bridge at which point he was travelling too fast and shot across the main road into a field. He limped home, wounded and covered in hen manure, at first to be chastised by Emily but then comforted as she became aware of the reasons behind his condition.

Cheet' never drove a car although he bought a Singer car for Roy on his seventeenth birthday. Joyce remembered that Roy had described the Singer's windows being operated by leather straps. The car had a petrol cut-off switch and when someone stole it one day they only travelled as far as Brough before it ran out of petrol and they had to abandon it.

Cheet's youngest brother Colin lived for a time on the Isle of Wight because his wife Amy had consumption and the kinder climate had been recommended as a cure. Sadly, Amy died in 1931 aged 31 years. Colin was taken on as a painter and decorator with Whitbread Breweries from 1931 to 1938. May Fletcher described how the whole Whitbread painting gang was sacked in 1938 as part of an efficiency drive and that the work was put out to contractors. From his home in Bradwell, Harry White, born 1909, told of himself, Colin Fletcher, Bill Seastron and Sew Cooke being interviewed at Earl's Cement works on the last day of 1938. All four were accepted and they started work on the same day, 2nd January 1939.

All in a day's work

Working at the Snake Inn on the A57 Sheffield to Glossop road

Cheet' taking a well earned drink

Cheet', second from right, assists with the installation of the bells at St Barnabas Church; 1938

Cheet', second from left, during installation of bells at St Barnabas Church; 1938. The young man on top of the bell, John Howe, later in his life carried out repairs to the inscriptions on Cheet's grave.

From left to right, Cheet, Noel, Jack and Colin outside Townend Joiners' Shop; circa 1939

Chapter 4
Second World War Including The Bradwell Home Guard

Notes of the Bradwell Home Guard, Bradwell A & B Sections; No 1 Platoon; A Company.

Company C.O.	Capt Hill of Bamford
2nd. in Command	1st. Lieut Baldwin, Bamford
Platoon C.O.	Lieut Price, Bamford
Ass. Platoon C.O.	Mr McKeen, Bamford
Qtr Sgt	Fox, Bamford
Orderly Rm. Sgt	Burgon, Bamford
Platoon C.O.	Jakeman, Castleton & Hope
Sgt SEN	C W Fletcher, Bradwell
Sgt JUN	G Thacker, Bradwell
Cpl SEN	J Ashbury, Bradwell (promoted Sgt. Nov. 1940)
Cpl JUN	R Charles, Bradwell
Cpl SEN	W Shirt, Bradwell
L/Cpl	F Nicholson, Bradwell (promoted Cpl. Nov. 1940)
L/Cpl	C Wain, Bradwell
L/Cpl	Rhodes, Bamford
L/Cpl	E Roberts, Bradwell

C Wain promoted L/Cpl Feb 1941.
M Grainger promoted L/Cpl Feb 1941.

I joined the Bradwell Section of the Home Guard in June 1940, was promoted Corporal in August then to Sergeant or Section Leader the same Month. We started doing Mobile Guards at Earles in June with 10 Men, each had a rifle, and enough cars to take us within appx 8 Miles radious, in case of Emergency. The Bradwell A Section consisted of these men:

C W Fletcher, Sgt	J Ashbury, Cpl	C Hawley
G Middleton	M Grainger	F Nicholson
W Revell (Jun)	H Bradwell	R Eyre
S Middleton	R Charles, Cpl	

Bradwell B Section consisted of these men:

G Thacker, Sgt	W Shirt, Cpl	E Roberts
R Wilson	R Revell	W Revell (Snr)
T O'Brien	R Fletcher	C Wain
C Bradwell	A Hallam	I Williamson
E Daniel	G Fletcher	N Fletcher
Joined Later:	G Daniel	P Skidmore

At First we did the Mobile Guard every 3 Nights. Then it got to every 5 Nights and now we go on every 8 Nights that means each Section. I am starting this diary in Aug 1940.

14-8-40; Myself and J Ashbury went Laying an Emergency Telephone Cable at Castleton from 6-30 P.M. untill 11-30 P.M. Same night myself, J Ashbury, Hedley Bradwell patroled Bradwell to see it was properly Blacked out untill 1-30 A.M. We had to warn several people about their lights.

23-8-40; Myself, J Ashbury, took the Sections on Hazlebadge Hills to give them Bombing instructions.

24-8-40; Myself, J Ashbury and C Hawley went to Castleton to Fix Telephone poles 10 A.M. to 1 P.M.

25-8-40; Parade at Messers Earles for Officers & N.C.Os. instructing them about different drills & Musketry as myself and Frank Poynton went to Derby on a refresher Course on drills Signalling & Musketry etc the week previous.

26-8-40; Self & Ashbury went down to Bamford Guard Room to fix a Trip Wire behind the Guard Rm. to save the Sentry patroling round Back of Guard Rm.

26-8-40; Myself, Ashbury, Thacker & Shirt each took 2 Men & patroled Bradwell looking for lights in Windows etc. We where armed with Rifles. I think it is the first time that Bradwell was ever patroled by Armed Men.

25-8-40; Sunday. Enemy planes came over & Bombed round Great Hucklow & Grindlow. Dropped appx 20 Bombs But did no damage except Killed 1 Fowle.

27-8-40; Myself, Thacker, Ashbury & Shirt took 4 Squads & opened out in Extended Order, accross Bradwell & Tideswell Moor to Search for a parashoot As it had been reported by the outpost Men on Winhill that they had seen one drop. We found nothing.

28-8-40; Home Guards went to Bamford to hear a Lecture by Col. Brook Taylor

29-8-40; Took our Sections on Hazlebadge Hills for Bombing Lessons

30-8-40; Laying Cable Hope & Castleton

31-8-40; Laying Cable Hope & Castleton

1-9-40; Laying Cable Brough to Bamford

2-9-40; Guard at Bamford alnight

3-9-40; Firing on Rifle Range under Wes School. Previous to this diary we fixed a rifle Range under the Wes Schoolroom

4-9-40; Rifle drill on Hazlebadge Hills both Sections.

5-9-40; Officers & N.C.Os looking round Bradwell for the best place for Strong posts or points. We decided My post be at bottom of Gore Lane the Council House & a road block just below nearer the Bath Hotel. Thackers post to be on Hazlebadge Hills with a road block in Bradwell Dale near the

Quarries. Ashburys to be at Crosslanes with patrols out Smalldale & patrol the Lane towards New Nook.

7-9-40; Sections turned out to Man the Strong points

8-9-40; Church parade the King & Queens day of prayer; appx 20 Men attended Night Service.

10-9-40; Our Section on Guard at Bamford all night.

11-9-40; Myself & Mr. Baldwin Laying Cable on Winhill

12-9-40; Drilling Sections in Memo. Hall; Rifle Drill; Capt Hill came & gave us an adress on disiplin

13-9-40; people in Council Houses warned to be ready to Move out in Case Hitler invaded our Country.

13-9-40; Rifle practice in Min Rifle Range; Report from Mrs. Brown the Council Houses Signalling during Air Raid Warning South of Bradwell Edge. Myself, Thacker, Ashbury & Fox went to investigate. Saw nothing.

14-9-40; Went to a Whist Drive in Memo Hall was fetched out half way through as the
Signalling was still going on we went South of Bradwell Edge untill 1 A.M. but saw nothing

15-9-40; Laying Cable from Winhill to Crookhill

16-9-40; Bombing practice at Bamford under the Company Bombing instructer, then went out untill 1 A.M. to try & locate the Signalling Saw nothing

17-9-40; Went out again after the Signalling

18-9-40; My Section on Guard at Bamford

19-9-40; Went round the Company Strong posts so that we should know where they where

20-9-40; Ashbury & Myself went out to find out the best route to lay Cable from Bradwell to Brough. Same night Ashbury & Myself fetched out to Bamford as phone wire had been cut.

21-9-40; Laying Cable Brough to Bradwell

22-9-40; Ashbury & Myself went with Mr. Baldwin & Mr. Price to lay Cable from Mam Tor post to bottom of Mam Tor

23-9-40; Laying Cable Brough to Bradwell

25-9-40; Rifles drill in Memo Hall Both Sections

26-9-40; My Section on Guard at Bamford

29-9-40; Sunday. Tactical Exersizes our Section acting Mobile Guard Reported Signalling West of Kiln Lane Earles sent men out to investigate. they saw 2 Men but they ran away, towards Smalldale

31-9-40; Firing on Rifle Range.

1-10-40; Drill in Memorial Hall. Critchlow of Berristor Lodge reported his Son Harry had found something off an Aeroplane. Myself, Cap Hill & Mr. Baldwin went to see it. it was off a German Stick of Bombs & it had been found on Bradwell Moor near Nicholsons top Barn

2-10-40; Firing on Rifle Range & Lecture by Cap Hill to N.C.Os.

4-10-40; My Section on Guard at Bamford

5-10-40; Wiring with Mr. Baldwin 2nd. in Command

6-10-40; Bradwell A & B Sections went to a Lecture at Bakewell

7-10-40; Overhauling Tel Cable Myself & Ashbury.

8-10-40; Drill in Memo Hall. We got our first Pay night from 3rd. Week in July. 3/- per night. I drew 6/- & gave it in to Coy Funds

9-10-40; Ashbury & Myself went to W. Vernons on Tideswell Moor. it was reported that Mr. Vernons daughter had found a Rod which was part of a stick of Bombs. When we got there, she had handed it into the police. She reported to us that a Mr. Critchlows Son of Whetson had found one of these Bomb sticks complete, so we went & had a look at it. It comprised of a Rod appx 3'6" Long x appx 1" in diam with a plate at one end about 12" x 8" which was padded.

9-10-40; Drill in the Memo Hall

13-10-40; Myself & Ashbury went to the Folly on Eccles on Tactical work. Du'Gard' Peach & Mr. Baldwin brough their Cinama Cameras & took a Moving picture of ourselves and other details from Home Guard.

15-10-40; Testing Tel Cables found same in Order.

16-10-40; Drill in Memo Hall. Called out untill Midnight as it was Thought Cable was Broken very wet night, so could not find Break.

17-10-40; Went out at night to try & Locate Break. (not Found)

18-10-40; Went out at night found the Break near Hope Bridge & repaired it in the dark.

19-10-40; Sat. Myself & Thacker took a party of Home Guard up to Bradwell dale Quarries we filled some of the Iron Waggons with Stone & Rubble and took same with iron rails down into the Dale ready to form a Road Block then took some down to the bottom of Gore Lane ready for another road Block.

20-10-40; Myself, Ashbury & R. Eyre went & overhauled part of the Telephone Cable, between Hope & Castleton. out 3.5 Hrs

20-10-40; Sunday. My Section on Guard at Company Guard Rm. at Bamford. Enemy Aircraft heard several Times between the Hours of 1 A.M. & 4 A.M. We heard 4 Bombs drop in Hathersage at 4 A.M. no Sirens went.

23-10-40; Drill in the Memo Hall.

24-10-40; Myself & J. Ashbury went to the Wes. Sunday School & fixed New Steel plate behind Targets & new pulleys etc

25-10-40; Wed. Drill in Memo Hall.

26-10-40; Working in rifle Range

26-10-40; Myself, Mr. Baldwin, went testing & repairing Telephone Cable between Brough & Hope Ashbury was with us

27-10-40; Both Bradwell Sections Marched from Bradwell Memo Hall and met remainder of Company at Travellers Rest then we all Marched up Aston Lane through Aston down the other Aston Lane on to Hope round Hope Church Back along the Main road to the Travellers then our Sections Marched back to Bradwell. we all enjoyed the March over 100 Men present.

29-10-40; My Section on Guard at Bamford

30-10-40; Wed. Bombing Lecture in Memo Hall.

2-11-40; Sat. Myself, Ashbury & R. Revell went to Mam Tor to repair phone Wire which had been broken in 3 or 4 places.

3-11-40; 10 Men from the Bradwell Home Guards went by Chara Motor with other Sections from Hope Castleton Bamford & Derwent, to Buxton & we heard a very interesting Lecture by O.C. Northern Command. Capt Hill in charge of our Company.

6-11-40; Drill in Memorial Hall both Sections.

7-11-40; Thursday. Our Section on Guard all night at Bamford.

10-11-40; I was in charge of Church parade we marched from the Memorial Hall to Bradwell Church for the Armistice Service appx 30 Home Guards present, Service at 3 P.M.

13-11-40; Drill in Memorial Hall & Lecture by E. Brown of Castleton on Scouting. both sections attended

16-11-40; My Section on Mobile Guard at Bamford.

16-11-40; Thomas Flintofts Funeral at Bradwell Church it was a Military Funeral & was attended by about 30 Home Guards. Marshall Elliott Blew the Last Post etc on his Bugle.

20-11-40; Drill & Lecture in Memo Hall both Sections present. Visited by Col. Wales & Col. Brook Taylor.

23-11-40; Sat. Myself, Ashbury & Mr. Baldwin went to Castleton & Tested Tel Cable, Then walked to Top of Win Hill to the O. Post & Tested the Wire enroute. Went at 9-15 A.M. arrived back at 1 P.M.

24-11-40; Sunday. myself, Shirt, Roberts & H Bradwell reported at Company Headquarters, Bamford. at 11 A.M. We then went on to Earles, with a Lewis Gun. We got into the Firing position. Then Mr. Du Gard Peach & Mr. Baldwin took our photoes, which are to be put in an Instruction Book. Arrived back home at 1 P.M.

25-11-40; My Section on Mobile Guard at Bamford. These Mobile Guards start at appx 7 P.M. & finish at 6.30 A.M. next morning.

27-11-40; Cleaning rifles in Drillhall & Lecture by Sgt Moore of Ashopton.

29-11-40; Firing on indoors rifle range young members of the Home Guard.

1-12-40; Sunday. Bradwell, Bamford & Derwent attacked. Hope & Castleton, Bradwell Sections proceeded Via Bradwell Dale, Coplow dale, Peak Forest on to the Winnates Farm. We parked Cars in the Winnates Farm yard, & then tried to take Castleton from the Winnates side. We got into Castleton but we were captured. Bamford Sections tried to take Hope &

Castleton from the Bamford side, this Failed. Derwent went up the Snake road, & came over the moors from Edale side this Failed. We had a good day & it was fine. Cpl Ashbury promoted to Sgt. Signaller; L/Cpl Nicholson promoted to Cpl a/s Section Leader to my Section.

2-12-40; Lecture in room over exservicemens club in Connection with the Tactical exersizes on the previous day. Offices, & N.C.Os. present only.

4-12-40; Wed. My Section on Mobile Guard at Bamford

7-12-40; Sat. out on Castleton route overhauling Telephone cable Myself, Ashbury & Mr. Baldwin.

11-12-40; Wed. Lecture in Memo Hall on Musketry by Mr. McKeen then we went to Bamford Institute to see a Cinama Show by Mr. Baldwin & L. Du Gard Peach.

12-12-40; Sheffield Bombed. Started about 7 P.M. & the Bombing lasted untill appx 4 A.M. next morning. The Sky seemed full of planes all night long.

15-12-40; Sun. Laying Telephone cable from Bradwell to Brough

15-12-40; Sheffield Bombed again

16-12-40; Our Section on Guard at Bamford
18-12-40; Drill in Memo. Hall both Sections.

22-12-40; Sun. Bradwell Sections Started 10-30 A.M. from drillhall for a Tactical Scheme on No. C. Strong point which is at the Cross Lane Villas which was defended by part of the Bradwell Section. The other part of the Sections where Supposed parashootists but we could not break through we finished at 12-30 P.M.

28-12-40; My Section on Mobile Guard at Bamford J. Ashbury in charge. I went with Sgt Thacker Cpl. Shirt & L/Cpl. Roberts to a Company Dinner, which was held at Yorkshire Bridge in Bamford.

29-12-40; Myself, J. Ashbury & R. Eyre relayed part of the Bradwell Telephone cable. Capt. Hill told me that I was posted as N.C.O. in sole charge of the Bradwell defences in case of an invasion by the Germans. we where instructed to be on the allert as the invasion was expected at any moment.

1941
5-1-41; Lecture on Lewis Gun in Memo Hall by L/C. E ROBERTS.

9-1-41; My Section on Mobile Guard at Bamford Bombs dropped at Dore & Totley & Buxton Area.

8-1-41; Lecture in Memo Hall by Mr. Price about expected invasion

11-1-41; Running about getting ready for Sand bag filling etc & Road Blocks.

12-1-41; Sunday. I was in Charge of a working of about 30 Men we went up to Windy, above Haddleton. We took a Lorry with us & Fill 5 or 600 Sand bags we left about 150 in various parts of the Village ready, in case any Incendary Bombs dropped in Bradwell. The other Sandbags we dumped near Bradwell Council Houses, & at Hills Stile, in readyness for our Strong points. We then went up to Bradwell dale Quarries for a load of Stone & Trolleys for a road Block & dumped same at Council Houses ready for Hitlers Invasion.

14-1-41; Order came through to issue rifle & 20 rounds of Ammunition to each member of the Home Guard, Who I thought was trained enough to use them. The people in Bradwell said we had done a very good & needy job when we took them the sandbags full of sand ready for any Incendary Bombs. There was 3 A. R. P. Posts in Bradwell. 1 on the Hills, 1 in Smalldale, & 1 at Stepen Middletons House up Hollow Gate. The Memorial Hall was ready for a first Aid Station. The fire Station was in a Garage Near Poyntons Shop. Mr. Ben Shirt was Chief A. R. P. Warden. Cyril Quince a/s Chief A. R. P. Warden. Mr. Applegate our Village policeman. Mr. Millard Sgt. of Special police.

15-1-41; Lecture in drillhall by Cpt Hill & Mr. Baldwin on Hitlers intended Invasion

17-1-41; Went to A Company headquarters at Bamford to the Company Meeting. All Section Leaders and a/s Section Leaders had to attend to hear the Company Business.

18-1-41; Sat. Myself, Ashbury, Grainger & H. Bradwell Started to make our advanced Strong point we Started to dig Trenches in the Field on the Left Side of the Sunken Road going down to Black Bridge Near the Bath Hotel. We started work at 9-30 A.M. & worked through to 4 P.M. We also decided to make a Lewis Gun post to the left of the old Bath Hotel.

18-1-41; The Bradwell Sections 3 & 4 had their dinner at the Bowling Green inn Smalldale. 24 members attended, Capt Hill, Mr Baldwin, Mr Price & Mr McKeen were Guests. We had a real Victorian dinner complete with the long Clay pipes. Dinner started at 7.30 P.M.

19-1-41; Sunday. Lecture on Lewis Gun in the Memorial Hall by L/c. E. Roberts, 12 Members attended

20-1-41; Monday. My Section Should have gone on Mobile Guard to Bamford but it was such a heavy Snow & still snowing hard the Guard was Cancelled. We kept getting fresh recruits. I had better name them, Bateman Eyre, Kenneth Fern, a youth called Webb who had been in the Army a few weeks but got his discharge & Leslie Bradwell.

22-1-41; Drill in Memorial Hall

24-1-41; Company meeting in Memo Hall about 30 officers & N.C.Os present.

25-1-41; Myself & Mr Baldwin went & had a look at our Strong points.

26-1-41; Sunday. Nos. 3 & 4 Sections, digging Trenches Near Bath Hotel & Hazelbadge Hills. Started 10 A.M. & Finished 4.30 P.M. about 12 Men turned up at each place. We found it heavy digging at the Bath Hotel as just under the Turf we struck Limestone Rock so we could not make a big show. On Hazlebadge Hills it was easy digging as it was Clay.

26-1-41; No. 4 Section Mobile Guard cancelled (Snowing).

27-1-41; Should have gone to Bamford to a Musketry Lecture, But it was cancelled.

28-1-41; Drill in the Memorial Hall for Nos. 3 & 4 Sections.

31-1-41; My Section on Mobile Guard at Bamford. I had to take 14 Men for Guard. Same night I left the Guard for 1.1/2 Hrs & went to the Coy. meeting.

1-2-41; Myself, Sgt Ashbury & Mr Baldwin went to Castleton & put a phone in at Sgt Moberley's house. At Night Myself & Sgt Ashbury went to Earles Home Guard dinner, which was held at the Bulls Head Hotel at Castleton, about 80 Members present.

2-2-41; Sunday. In the morning I took a party of Earles men up to Cross Lane's post & instructed them what to do. After, my section went digging Trenches at Bath Hotel & Sgt Thackers section under Cpl Shirt went Trench digging on Hazlebadge Hills. Cap. Hill & Mr Baldwin came & inspected our Trenches.

3-2-41; Lecture on Musketry by Mr. McKeen. Capt Hill & Mr Baldwin present at Lecture. Went on Hazlebadge Hills to examine S Point.

6-2-41; Myself, W. Shirt & Mr. McKeen took 7 youths on Miniture Rifle Range for Course of Firing they fired very well.

7-2-41; Went to Company office, at Bamford to Company meeting. Capt Hill was promoted to 2nd. in Command of the Battalion.

8-2-41; Mr. Baldwin came up to see me & we went up to Crosslane Strong point, and decided where to dig Slip Trenches, & put a road Block. The road block to be at the top of Hungry Lane. We decided that the slip Trenches should be in John Fletchers field at the bottom of Haddleton.

9-2-41; Sunday. My Section went down to the Bath Hotel to clean our Headquarters out which is a loft in one of the outbuildings. After dinner we went digging Trenches near the Bath Hotel. Thackers Section where out on Hazlebadge digging trenches, (It was a very wet day.)

10-2-41; Lecture on Musketry by Mr. McKeen about 30 Bradwell home Guards present.

11-2-41; My Section on Mobile Guard at Bamford 13 men present we manned Win Hill post. I was instructed to get Women Cooks in case we had to man our Strong points, & to find Cooking and sleeping accomodation at each S. point. I went & saw Mrs. Hayes & she soon got the Women Volunteers for Cooking. Here are their Names. Mrs. Hayes, Mrs. Millard, Mrs. Fischer, Miss Fischer, Mrs. Doug Bradwell, Mrs. H. Mabbott, Mrs. Earle, for Bath Hotel S. point. Mrs. Rowland, Miss Lily Morton, Mrs. Sanderson, Mrs. L. Hall, Mrs. S. Wood, Mrs. B. Wragg for CrossLane post. Mrs. Bromage, Mrs. Geo. Smith, Mrs. Bossingham, Mrs. R. Bennett, Mrs. B. Walker Hills Stile Strong point.

12-2-41; Ten Home Guards went firing on Min Rifle Range.

13-2-41; I had orders to go round to the Shops in Bradwell & find out if the Shop keepers could supply Rations, for appx 100 Home Guards, to supply them with rations for 5 Days in case of Emergency. A. F. Hancock Ltd & The Co'op stated they would undertake the Job.

11-2-41; Volunteer M. Grainger promoted to Lance Corporal.

14-2-41; Went down to Company meeting at Bamford Myself, Thacker & Shirt. Capt Hill was promoted to Sec. in Command to the Battalion.

16-2-41; Sunday. Section Leaders in our Company went to Earles for instructions in drill etc. Bradwell Sections turned out for Trench digging. I went after dinner to dig but Mr. Price, &, McKeen came up & I had to go & Show them our Strong points. it was a fine morning but later it turned out very wet with rain & Sleet.

17-2-41; Drill & Lecture in the Memo Hall, Mr. McKeen came to Bradwell & gave us a Lecture on the Rifle which was very interesting, about 20 Members present. Sgt Thackers Section on Guard at Bamford.

20-2-41; Cpl Shirt took some of our new Members on the Miniture Range for Shooting.

21-2-41; Went to Bamford to company meeting

22-2-41; My Section went to Bamford on Mobile Guard. 14 Bradwell men on duty. We had a quite night.

23-2-41; Both Bradwell Sections out digging Trenches at Bath Hotel & Hazlebadge Hills Mr. McKeen came up to see us.

24-2-41; Drill & lecture in the Memo Hall by Mr. McKeen

25-2-41; Myself, Thacker & Shirt went up to Tideswell to get in Contact with their Home Guards. We saw Mr. Palfreyman & Cpl Sellars & we each made several notes, So as we could get in touch with one another in case an emergency arose.

26-2-41; Our Company Sgt Major Poynton came up to Bradwell from Bamford, for me to go round our Strong points with Him.

28-2-41; Company Meeting at Bamford. I did not go I was Ill. I was asked to be 2nd. in Comd. to No. 4 platoon, But refused.

2-3-41; Sunday. Both Sections digging at Strong points.

3-3-41; Monday. Drill in Memo Hall. Both Sections present.

5-3-41; My Section on Mobile Guard at Bamford I did not go owing to illness

6-3-41; Mr. McKean brought one of Bamford Sections to Shoot on the indoor rifle range.

4-3-41; Company Meeting at Bamford I did not go owing to illness.

9-3-41; Sunday. The Battalion where detailed to go up to Earles quarries, to see how to lay a Land mine with high explosives, to Blow tanks up but it was cancelled owing to very bad weather.

10-3-41; Drill in the Memo Hall both Sections

11-3-41; Tuesday. Sgt Thackers Section went on Mobile Guard. I was asked again if I would take a Commission either 2nd. in Command of No. 4 platoon which consists of Messers Earles men, or if I would take 2nd. in Command of No. 1 platoon. I refused as I did not want the Job.

12 & 13-3-41; Bradwell Home Guards went firing on the Miniture rifle range, their firing was very good. Mr. McKean came up to my house & we had a good talk on Various things re the Home Guard.

14-3-41; Meeting at Bamford Company H.Q. I did not go as I was Ill.

16-3-41; My Section on Guard at Bamford the Company went up to Coats Green to see a demonstration on Tank Traps and different kinds of Bombs etc. there was 3 very heavy explosions I believe it was a very good Show, & a very good turn out of the Home Guards. appx. 250 Men

18-3-41; New orders came through to take 6 Rifle men & four Lewis Gun men on the Mobile Guard instead of the 14 Men.

20-3-41; New Orders came through to work a Dawn patrol Consisting of Two Men & the Orderly Officer, this patrol starts at 5 A.M. To 7 A.M. those men are detailed to go either up to Winhill or Mam Tor between 5 A.M. & 7 A.M. This is the message which I received from our platoon Commander.

A Coy Home Guard 1st. Battalion. No. 1 platoon From No. 1 O/C To Sgt CWFletcher Bradwell: (1) Commencing Thursday, March 20, Dawn patrol will Maintain Observation over the Company Area. (2) For the period March 20th. untill Further Notice the patrols will stand to at 05'00 hrs and Stand down at 07-00 hrs. (3) These patrols will consist of 2 Men and the Orderly officer, And will cover the Hope Valley and Surrounding Hills, from a position of Vantage on Mam Torr, or Win Hill. (4) The Rendevous for the Bradwell patrols will be the memo Hall You will Supply two Men on each of the Following Dates. Sat March 22nd; CWFletcher and H. Bradwell; Frid March 28, other men to be detailed.

21-3-41; Company Meeting at Bamford.

22-3-41; Sgt Thackers Section on Mobile patrol. We take 10 Men again instead of 14.

23-3-41; Bradwell 3 & 4 Sections went by Car to Bamford Church it was day of National prayer They started from Bradwell at 10 AM.

24-3-41; Nos. 3 & 4 Sections had Kit inspection in the Memorial Hall Mr. McKean took the parade.

27-3-41; My Section on Mobile Guard at Bamford & 2 men on dawn patrol

28-3-41; Company meeting at Bamford

27-3-41; Bombs dropped near Coplowdale

29-3-41; Dance for Home Guard comforts fund in the Memorial Hall from 7-30 to 10-45 P.M. Members of Home Guard wore uniform.

29-3-41; Sgt Ashbury & part of No. 3 & 4 Sections out Wiring

31-3-41; Monday. Lecture on Gas, by Dr. Mary Andrews for Bradwell Nos. 3 & 4 Sections in the Memorial Hall, We also had Gas Mask drill, I was drilling the Home Guards with our Gas Masks on. Everybody enjoyed both the Lecture & Drill about 30 Home Guards present

APRIL 2nd; Sgt Thackers Section on Mobile Guard at Bamford.

4-4-41; Friday. Company meeting at Bamford.

6-4-41; Trench digging at Strong points Both Sections.

7-4-41; My Section on Mobile Guard at Bamford. The Germans dropped Bombs; appx 7 at or near Coplow dale.

11-4-41; Orders came through for Roy Eyre & R. Revill each to be promoted to L/Corporal and E. Roberts to be promoted to Full Corporal

13-4-41; Sunday. Sgt Thackers Section on Mobile Guard at Bamford, Noel & Roy Fletcher on dawn patrol

18-4-41; Frid. My Section on Mobile Guard at Bamford. Sgt Ashbury & H. Bradwell on dawn patrol. & Company meeting.

20-4-41; Sunday. Myself, Mr. McKean, Shirt & Thacker went up to Coplowdale to get in touch with the Search light Battery we had a good look round the Search lights & it was very interesting. In the afternoon I went with my Section, working on our Strong points.

21-4-41; Drill in the memorial Hall. Gas Drill & Lecture by Dr. Mary Andrews of Shatton. She gave us a very interesting Lecture on Gas. I will just make a note on our Dawn patrols; the orderly Officer & 2 Men are Detailed every Morning at appx 04'30 hrs or 05'30 hrs they go by Car as far as Thornhill or Mam Tor then climb to the Top of either of these Hills for Observation purposes. If Visability is bad they patrol through different Villages by Car & on the edge of the Moors. They go out in case any parashoots should Land then they should notify the Mobile Guard who would rush up by Car to get in action against them.

21-4-41; 6 of the Home Guard Volunteers, Volunteered to Help the Bradwell Red Cross unit in Case Bradwell was Bombed these are their names: Hedley Bradwell, Kenneth Fern, Noel Fletcher, Cyril Bradwell, George Rowland, Cheetham William Fletcher. We each filled a form up to help Mrs. Hayes Bradwell Redcross Township Leader. This does not interfere with Home Guard Duties.

24-4-41; Thackers Section on Mobile Guard at Bamford. The Section had to go up to Shatton Moor at Night as some fool had set the Gorse on fire, & it was dangerous, as the Enemy Aircraft might see it.

25-4-41; The Bombing Officer came up to Bradwell with a Load of Bombs, they stored them in the Cavern in Bradwell Dale. This Cavern belonged to Mrs. Harry Walker.

27-4-41; Sunday. We went down to Hope & each Bradwell member of the Home Guard went through the Gas Van which consisted of Tear Gas. Not one Gas Mask was found to be faulty. Dr. Mary Andrews was in attendance. In the Afternoon went working on our Strong Points.

28-4-41; Bradwell 3 & 4 Sections went up to Hazlebadge & we did a Tactical Exersize in the Evening. Mr. McKean took Charge.

29-4-41; My Section on Mobile Guard at Bamford. The R.S.M. gave us a demonstration on the Tommy Gun. We had never handled a Tommy Gun before. The RSM told us we were going to be issued with them.

30-4-41; Messers Earles disbanded their Home Guard as a platoon, Owing to Mr. Davis the Manager leaving the district, he was in Command of Them. It was decided to make a platoon in Bradwell

2-5-41; Friday. Meeting at Bath Hotel Consisting Mr. Fiennes new platoon officer & Section Leaders and A/S. Section Leaders to form a Conbine Earles & Bradwell Sections into 1 platoon

3-5-41; Sat. Myself & Ashbury went up to Winhill Post & Repaired Beds etc & Cleaned the post out.

4-5-41; Training Volunteers in Lewis Gun Drill..

5-5-41; Scheme & attack on the Bath Hotel Strong Point by Nos. 3 & 4 Sections. Our Sections Started to man Winhill post during the night.

7-5-41; Myself & 3 Men on Winhill O.P. Enemy planes overhead to about 3 oclock in the Morning. The O.Ps. are manned from 8 PM untill 6 AM.

8-5-41; Section Leaders went to Mr. Fiennes who was appointed our platoon Commander, to discuss various things to improve our platoon from this date. our platoon is No. 4 & my section altered to No. 13 Section, & Sgt Thackers Section to No. 14 Section. It was decided that the Mobile Guard should be manned at Bradwell from this date, & the room to be in the primitive Methodist Sunday School in Hugh Lane.

10-5-41; Myself, Sgt Ashbury went & put the phone into the Hope New Guard room, & the phone in the Methodist Sunday School ready for My Section mounting Guard on Monday.

11-5-41; Sunday. Myself, Mr. Baldwin, Mr. Fiennes & W. Shirt went up Hadleton on to Windy to find a new place as observation post, instead of going up to Win Hill. We found a place near Hartle Moor Lane, a stone Built place belonging to Messers Hodkin & Jones. We decided to have same. The same day in the afternoon we went on Church parade, with the Searchlight unit from Coplowdale & other Organizations.

12-5-41; My Section on Mobile Guard in the new Guard Room in the P.M. Sunday School

13-5-41; Fixing the phone Wire from our O.P. on Windy to our new Guard Room

15-5-41; Bradwell Edge was Covered with Snow & we had frost during the night.

16-5-41; fixing the phone wire from Windy to Bradwell from the Windy O.P.

17-5-41; Myself, Sgt Ashbury, Cpl Grainger, Cpl Roberts, H. Bradwell went with lorry to Winhill to move beds etc from Winhill to Windy. We also fixed Stove & beds in the Windy new O.P.

18-5-41; Myself & 3 Men went & manned the New Windy O.P. we had a very warm quite night. Mr. Baldwin, Price, & their Wives came up to see us.

18-5-41; We moved the Stores from Earles to Bradwell New Guard room, in the Morning, & in the Afternoon we had Lewis Gun Drill on Hazlebadge Hills. Mr. Baldwin took some Cinamalagtake photoes of us. I was on Windy O.P. all night

19-5-41; Monday. Roy Joined the Navy & went to Portsmouth.

19-5-41; Talk & Lecture by Mr. Fiennes our new platoon Commander in our new Guard room at the P.M. Chapel.

20-5-41; Promoted to platoon Sgt Major CWFletcher

21-5-41; Mr. Fiennes came up to my house & we went up to Windy post, we found only 3 Men on duty instead of 4. The Sentry did not challenge us, this was not in order & Mr. Fiennes gave them a good talking too. We also found 2 part bottles of Beer in the post. I was pleased it was not my Section.

25-5-41; The Home Guard had a Tactical exersise with the Military, Who attacked our Road Blocks. The Military threw Tear Gas bombs at us

26-5-41; Myself & 3 Men on Windy post all night.

28-5-41; My Section on Mobile Guard at Bradwell all night.

1-6-41; Whit Sunday. My Section had to Mount mobile Guard owing to No 16/17 Section failing to turn up for duty. These men turned out for Duty:- E. Roberts, J. Ashbury, L. Bradwell, R. Eyre, H. Bradwell, R. Revill, B. Eyre, G. Daniel, CWFletcher.

3-6-41; My Section on O.P. at Windy.

4-6-41; I took about 20 Home Guards up in Bradwell Dale Quarries & gave them Some musketry drill.

7-6-41; 14 Bradwell Home Guards went to Edale Rifle Range on Firing course. Below are their scores. (I fired with Tommy Gun.)

C W	Fletcher	20 points out of 25.
N.	Fletcher	23 points
G.	Fletcher	20 points
A.	Burrows	19 points
B.	Eyre	18 points
G.	Daniel	19 points
E.	Roberts	16 points
	Ramsdale	16 points
G.	Rowland	16 points
Hugh	Bradwell	15 points
R.	Boyes	14 points
G.	Thacker	14 points
G.	Williams	14 points
	TOTAL	224 points

7-6-41; Sat. My Section on Windy O.P.

8-6-41; We had a Tour round Strong points.

9-6-41; Digging bank out in Bradwell dale for By pass for Tanks etc near Road Block.

10-6-41; Working party in Bradwell dale

11-6-41; In Charge of Working party in Bradwell dale.

12-6-41; Myself and J. Ashbury up Mam Tor wiring

13-6-41; My Section on Mobile Guard at Bradwell

14-6-41; Sat. 4 Men from each Section firing at Edale rifle Range. Lewis Gunners fired a Course

15-6-41; Sunday. N.C.O.s went on to Hazlebadge Hills for Drill under Mr. Fiennes our O.C. platoon.

16-6-41; I took some of the new members in rifle Drill in the Guard Room.

19-6-41; We had a demonstration, & Lecture on the Tommy Gun, by a Sergeant from the York & Lancs. Reg.

21-6-41; We went to Edale to fire a Rifle course. Myself & 10 Men with Hancocks Chara. We all Fired well. I got 22 points out of 25.

21-6-41; Firing Scores at Edale by the Bradwell H.G.s. Sgt CW. Fletcher 22 points, Sgt Thacker 14, K. Fern 12, Geo. Fletcher 21, R. Revill 15, Sgt Ashbury 7, L. Bradwell 17, C. Hawley 15, N. Fletcher 11, H. Bradwell 23, A. Fathers 22. Some of these Men had not fired before.

22-6-41; My Section & Sgt Thackers Section went up to Hazlebadge Hills in the afternoon, & did some signalling Drill, we had to pack up owing to a severe Thunder Storm.

23-6-41; My Section & Sgt Thackers Section went working up Bradwell dale on Road Block.

25-6-41; It was reported that a Land Mine was dropped up Woodlands. One of our Spitfires was after the German Bomber about 1-30 AM. Wed. Morning that this happened. No damage was done. The parashoot was found about 100 Yards away from the Bomb Crater & it was perfect. Mr. Baldwin came up and asked me to be platoon Commander over No. 4 platoon. I did not want to take a Commission.

29-6-41; All Sections went on Hazlebadge Hills for drill. My Section Mobile Guard

30-6-41; Monday. Working on Bradwell dale road Block

2-7-41; Working on Bradwell dale road block.

July 3rd; Myself & Major Baldwin went up to Coplowdale to have a look round Searchlight Batteries.

5-7-41; Went to Edale Rifle Range with a Section of Home Guards

6-7-41; Took platoon to Hazlebadge Hills for drill. At night we went to Castleton to see home Guard Film.

7-7-41; 15, 16/17 Sections Transfered to Mine, & Sgt Thackers Sections. Working on Bradwell dale Road Block. We had a lot of excavating to do

9-7-41; Working on Bradwell dale Road Block. Some of the platoon went to Castleton to see a Tank Film

11-7-41; My Section on Mobile Guard at Bradwell

13-7-41; Sunday. Training on Hazlebadge Hills.

14-7-41; Firing practice in Bradwell dale Quarries.

16-7-41; Firing practice in Bradwell dale Quarries.

19-7-41; Sat. My Section Mobile Guard at Bradwell

20-7-41; Training on Hazlebadge Hills

21-7-41; Firing practice on indoor Range

23-7-41; Firing practice up Bradwell dale

27-7-41; We had a platoon Tactical Exercise on Windy O.P. Everybody enjoyed it. My Section on Mobile Guard at Night

28-7-41; Monday. Eleven men & myself made a Sham Attack on Hathersage. We Started our Attack at 8-40 P.M. from Bretton Clough, it was a pouring wet night & every one of us got drenched through. When we arrived at Hathersage we found that their Home Guards had Cancelled it. The Bradwell lads enjoyed it but it was disapointing when the Hathersage lads did not turn out.

30-7-41; We went out & had a look round our Strong point.

Aug. 2nd; Sat. Myself & Thacker went to Stoke Hall on a General, Home Guard Course.
About Midnight I went up to Windy post to see if the men where O.K.

3-8-41; Went to Stoke Hall on Second Course

4-8-41; Went to Stoke Hall for Third Course then went on Mobile Guard all night.

6-8-41; Wed. The platoon went to Castleton to the Peak Pavillion to see a Film on Home Guard Tactics, A platoon in Attack & Defence.

10-8-41; Sunday. We had a Company Tactical Exercise. I was in Charge of the Bradwell platoon of about 20 Men, not a bad turn out. We met at Bradwell Guard Room at 9-30 AM. proceeded by Motor Bus to Derwent. We left the Bus & deployed in 3 Sections towards Asopton, which was our Objective. The Defence of Ashopton was very good. We heard that Mr. Fiennes had resigned as platoon Comr. of our platoon.

11-8-41; We had a pay night for our platoon in the Guard Room.

12-8-41; Tues. My Section on Mobile Guard at Bradwell Guard Room. The Sirens went at 5 past midnight and lasted for about 2 Hrs. Myself & Ashbury went to Brough to repair a break in the phone Wire

13-8-41; Drill night Cpl E. Roberts gave us Lewis Gun instructions & Drill.

14-8-41; Thurs. Mr. Baldwin came up to see me about reorganizing our platoon owing to Mr. Fiennes leaving the District. We had a long Talk & he left things in my hands. E. Roberts promoted from Cpl to Sgt; W. Shirt promoted from Cpl to Musketry Sgt; R Boyes promoted from L/Cpl to Sgt in Charge of my Section; L/Cpl Wain promoted to Cpl; Volunteer W. Marsden promoted to L/Cpl Bomber.

17-8-41 to Oct 5th 1941; I havent had much time to enter notes in this Ledger between these days. But a lot has gone off. We have had a few Schemes, and Tactical Exercises. We made a Tactical exercise on Ashopton and one on Hathersage. We had a 18 hr stand to on our Action Stations. We got 100 per cent praise, the women cooks were at Action Stations. We lost 2 good officers. Mr. McKean got killed on a Motor Cycle, Mr. Pryce died a week after. On the 5th of Oct 1941 (Sunday) the other platoons made an attack on Bradwell. We manned action Stations at 10-30 AM. on the above date. It was a very good try out, but Visability was very bad for our Scouts. Anyway the Bradwell platoon got praise for their defensive scheme. The A.R.P. and Firemen, Ambulence men, nurses, and fire spotters were all on the job. Bradwell Lewis gun teams got highly praised.

HOME GUARD VOLUNTEERS RESIDING IN BRADWELL

J. S.	ASHBURY	old post office
H. S.	BRADWELL	Bridge End
C.	BRADWELL	Towngate
L. S.	BRADWELL	Towngate
R. A.	CHARLES	Towngate
H. H.	CRITCHLOW	Burnstall Lodge Farm
E.	DANIEL	Towngate
G.	DANIEL	Towngate
R.	DUTTON	Towngate
R.	EYRE	14 Council Houses
B.	EYRE	Church Street
J.V.E.	EASTON	Hallowgate
C. W.	FLETCHER	Townend
R.	FLETCHER	Townend
N. H.	FLETCHER	Dialstones
G.J.L.	FLETCHER	Dialstones

K.	FERN	*Towngate*
B. M.	GRAINGER	*New Nook*
C. J.	HAWLEY	*Tor Top*
C.	MARSHALL	*"Ingledene"*
G.	MIDDLETON	*The Hills*
F. F.	NICHOLSON	*Glen View*
T.	O'BRIEN	*Elm Tree Cottage*
W. E.	PASHLEY	*Brookside Garage*
W. C.	REVILL	*Paradise Farm*
W. H.	REVILL	*Nether Side*
R. A.	REVILL	*Nether Side*
E.	ROBERTS	*Townend*
W. H.	SHIRT	*New Church Street*
G.	THACKER	*Nether Side*
C. P.	WAIN	*Church St.*
I.	WILLIAMSON	*Dale End*
A. G.	ROWLAND	*Church St.*
I.	BOTTOMLEY	*The Hills*
A.	FATHERS	*The Hills*
C. T.	ALLEN	*5 Dale End*
C. H.	ALLEN	*Hill Head*
F.	ANDREW	*Church St.*
C. W.	ANDREW	*Dialstones*
C. E.	ARNOLD	*Stretfield*
H. L.	ASHMORE	*Smithy Hill*
Hugh	BRADWELL	*16 Council Houses*
D. R.	BAKER	*Brough*

R.	BENNETT	*Jeffery Lane*
A. A.	BURROWS	*Smithy Hill*
D.	BROADBENT	*The Hills*
D.	BRADWELL	*5 Gore Lane*
T.	BROWN	*Brook Buildings*
T. R.	BUXTON	*Church Street*
T. M.	COOPER	*Hill Head*
S.	COOKE	*Towngate*
D.	DAKIN	*Smalldale*
S. A.	DAKIN	*Hollowgate*
A.	DANIEL	*Towngate*
A. J.	DITCHMAN	*Brough*
W.	ELLIOTT	*Smalldale*
T. W.	ELLIOTT	*Church St.*
Colin	FLETCHER	*Yard End*
L.	FLACK	*Town Gate*
W.	FLINTOFT	*Smithy Hill*
H. A.	GOODISON	*Church Street*
H.	GREGORY	*The Hills*
A.	GIBSON	*Bessie Lane*
R.	HALL	*Smalldale*
H.	HODGKINSON	*Smalldale*
R.	HALLAM	*Smithy Hill*
H. M.	MILLER	*The Gutter*
H.	HART	*Church Street*
J.	HOARE	*Church Street*
J. R.	HOARE	*The Hills*

H.	HOWE	Towngate
T.	HOWELL	Hill Head
F.	JONES	Church Street
E.	JONES	Smalldale
E.	JACKLIN	Town Gate
J.	JOHNSON	Smalldale
		3 Gore Lane
F.	KAY	Smalldale
H. W.	LEE	Woodcroft
F. P.	LIVERSIDGE	Towngate
W. H.	McLELLAN	The Hills
S.	MIDDLETON	Hill Head
W.	MARSDEN	Hugh Lane
J. C.	OLLERENSHAW	Irongate
A.	PONSONBY	Gore Lane
J. R.	POYNTON	Bridge Street
G. W.	PARRITT	Far Hill
G.	POOLE	Hill Head
G.	ROBERTS	Fox Lane
L. W.	ROBINSON	Smalldale
J.	RUDD	Outland Head
A.	ROBINSON	Smithy Hill
J. W.	RAMSDALE	Smithy Hill
S.	REPTON	19 Council Houses
E.	ROBERTS	4 Gore Lane
G.	SAXON	New Council Houses
J. W.	SEASTRON	Hill Head

J. W.	SYKES	Smalldale
S. S.	SMITH	24 Council Houses
G. A.	STRAW	Dialstones
G.	SLATER	Church Street
A.	THOMPSON	Mitchlow Lane
T. F.	TOWERS	The Hills
H. F.	TOWNSEND	Smalldale
M. J.	TOBIN	12 Gore Lane
A. E.	TAYLOR	Smithy Hill
M.	URWIN	Smalldale
E.	WILLIAMS	Michlow Lane
H.	WHITE	Far Hill
A. H.	WEAVER	Lynhurst, The Hills

Noel Fletcher recounted a story which involved Cheet', thus: Arthur Hallam, who was related to Cheet's mother Annie, was in the Home Guard and subsequently enlisted in the Navy. Cheet' had always impressed on Arthur the need to keep secret any details of his training, location, ships, etc. On one occasion when Arthur was on leave Cheet' asked him "where are you now then?" to which Arthur replied "at the seaside!"

George Parritt recalled "Cheet' was in charge of us in the Home Guard because of his earlier experiences in WW1. He drilled us and put us right". Previously the Home Guard had been Local Defence Volunteers, LDV, whom Lord Haw Haw had referred to as 'Look, Duck and Vanish'. Lord Haw Haw, real name William Joyce, was hanged in 1946 having been found guilty of treason. George Parritt remembered manning Observation Posts at Winhill and Windy, the latter being up Haddleton to the right of

Hoveringham's Quarry. Windy had been an old barn belonging to Hodkin & Jones and later was used as a weighbridge.

Remembering his Home Guard experiences Harry White of Bradwell described camping at Coplowdale. "We had some rum times. Bill Seastron, Bill Oldfield, me and another chap, whose name I can't remember, used to play brag - it was the only time I'd ever played cards. One night we went to the Bulls Head at Little Hucklow for a few pints followed by pie and peas for supper; later, in the tent we played brag all night by candlelight because of the blackout". He remembered Cheet' as sergeant in the Home Guard, "a biggish, well-made chap" and recalled "we used to march at night over the moors. Two of us had to go on fire guard in the quarry during the war." Harry also remembered incendiary bombs landing on the tarmac plant in Stoney Middleton dale and putting it out of action.

Tom Buxton, aged 92 years, of Hope remembered Cheet' as "a very popular fellow - a character". He recalled that Cheet' along with Ernest Elliott, Sailor Sam, Billy Oldfield and others, used to congregate at the bridge over Bradwell brook on the main road.

Speaking of the Home Guard Tom offered the opinion that "some of the senior officers were a bit too big for their boots!" In describing the Home Guard Tom often mentioned Billy Shirt who is listed in Cheet's journal as a senior corporal. Many people will remember Bill Shirt as the man who ran the well stocked clothing shop at Town Bottom. Bill Shirt used to draw on Tom's army experience and knowing the pitfalls of drilling inexperienced volunteers would say "just march us down through the village will you Tom?"

Tom recalled "We had wooden rifles and used to go up Bradwell Dale to the space in front of Morton's quarry where we did arms drill. The only proper rifles were at Earls' HQ but we had no live ammunition or even blanks to practise with. I was able to provide some 'safe' bullets for loading practise but I always collected them up afterwards. Someone else also provided a few bullets for practise, saying that they were 'safe', but one of them went off with a right bang. It's pure luck no-one was injured - it goes to show how dangerous some of the Home Guard stuff was."

Amongst many other recollections Tom described the funeral of Thomas Flintoft. He went on to say "Bill Shirt and others wanted to give Thomas a full military funeral and they asked me if I'd train them on arms drill and presenting arms. I guided them towards something a bit less ambitious and suggested that an orderly line of men, stood to attention on each side of the Church drive, would suffice." Cheet's journal entry for 16 November 1940 confirms Thomas Flintoft as having a military funeral at Bradwell Church attended by about 30 Home Guards.

Cheet's diary entry for 25 August 1940 was supported by the 30 August 1940 edition of the Derbyshire Times which carried the headline "No Casualties - Futile Bombing: cat killed, cow wounded". Reporting on bombs dropped in rural areas the article quoted one farmer as saying "if you ask me, the sightseers we had later in the day did far more damage than the bombs".

The Derbyshire Times dated Friday 20 December 1940 corroborated his entries for 12 and 15 December regarding the bombing of Sheffield. An article headed "Sheffield Full of Courage, Inhabitants Show Great Pluck in Terrible Ordeal" went on to say "Though her face is badly scarred by the enemy attacks which lasted for 11 hours last Thursday night and for a considerable period on Sunday evening also, Sheffield's heart is still full of courage; her spirit is undaunted".

Roy and Joyce - early days

Noel Fletcher

George Fletcher

Chapter 5
Further Poems With Jokes And Tales From Bradwell And Roundabout

A FEW LINES FROM THE TRENCHES
by C W Fletcher

Our hearts' with our Mothers, Sweethearts or Wives
While we are out Fighting abroad
We are Guarding you all, at the risk of our Lives
With our Rifles our Bayonetts & Swords
We are Happy contented tho plenty of work
But soon we shall write you a line
And when we are using our Guns & our dirks
We'll be thinking of Home o'er the Brine
We are up to our Knees in the Slush & the Mud
The Shells, roaring over our Heads
We could do with a Wash, by using some Suds
And could do, with a Sleep, in our Beds
Those Fags that you sent, We thank you so much
The cake that you made, was so nice
We think of the Fire, Burning bright in the Hearth
When we are busy catching the Lice
Old Hitler'll be busy, when he makes his Attack
He will find, we're as good as our Dads
In 1914, our Pa's did not Lack,
the Spirit, thats born in us Lads

UNTITLED

I think its time we had a change
two wars, both, in our time
I wish old Hitler could have the mange
and not be worth a dime

Its very well for German folk
to follow Hitler's plea
They ought to put him in a yoke
and throw him in the sea

His brains are wool his head is swelled
that bomb was just too late
Its time old Ribbentoff was helled
and both left to their fate

Old Hess and Goering, should both be tarred
then should be stewed in oil
A pair they'd make, some damn good lard
then throw it on the soil

Old Hitler old Hitler he's worse than old Nick
he daren't leave his den without guards
We'd put round his neck a rope with a brick
or burn him, like an old pack of cards.

UNTITLED

Now if you tune into, Haw Haw
You'll Hear a fool, Caw Caw
You'll think it is an old, Saw Saw
That's got a Bad Flaw Flaw
You See that Chap he has some Jaw
Sometimes I think he's Straw
You see that man is just a Flaw
England is looking For
He's Titled with the name of Lord
His Neck is ready for the Sword
Perhaps be better with a cord
I'm sure he has us Bored
I think it's time we had him Floored
or if we had him Moored
perhaps some would like him Gored
Or chained up in a Ford.

UNTITLED

My Boy has gone, across the pond
And left me alone, at Home
He just Knows I'm very fond
And will write across the Foam

He's only young, not Twenty one
I hope he will take care

(unfinished)

THE MISER'S HOARD

Ha, Ha, Ha, Ha, Ha, Ha, Ha,
My Gold, My Gold, My Gold,
I count it every night
Nobody Knows, no, Nobody Knows
where I hide my gold at night.

BRADWELL MUNITION WORKS AT THE NEWBURGH

Just a line, about these Works
placed on the Netherside
The Ladies there, don't wear Skirts
But work in Overalls.
You see them go, for Eight each Morn
Relief goes Eight each Night.

(unfinished)

THE GRANDFATHER CLOCK, by C W FLETCHER

It stands in a corner covered with dust
And I've looked at it Hundreds of times.
I think that if Grandpa hadn't a crust
He wouldn't part with the Clock that chimes
Its face is of Brass its finger of Steel
And its case is of good English oak
for when the hour strikes you should hear the peal
of the Bell in the Wooden Cloak
Grandpa says its two Hundred years old
And he can tell the time to a tick
That neither Rubies, Jewels nor anyone's Gold
Would buy it as its been such a Brick.
It must stand in its corner as long as I live
Then he says he will leave it to me
So I shall Cling, as my names Olive
To the Clock thats mine to be
I shall take Great care of Grandpa's Clock
It shall stop where its always Been
I shall always listen to its Grand Tick Tock
It shall stand where its always seen.

Cheet' had a great love for clocks and Grace used to describe to her grandson how he was always buying extra ones. He used to spend lots of time setting them all to the same time and trying to get them chiming together.

THE OLD BRADWELL LEAD MINERS

The Lead Miners worked, with picks and spades
And they left their marks behind
If a Walk you take, before night Fades
Lumps of Lead, no doubt you'll find
Those miners they worked, for paltry pounds
At least Fourteen Hours a day
They must have done, if you look at those Mounds
Of Gravel in heaps I say.
I've heard people say, their Wives did Work
As hard, as the Miners themselves
Up in a morning, they did not Shirk
Nor near the Fire, did they Dwell
They helped with the Hotch, & also the winch
They'd no time, for powder & paint
But did their work, without a Hinch
Today, the Girls would Faint.
Their little clay pipes I've often seen
And they liked their pinches, of Snuff
But I do believe, the lead was Clean
When it handed, down to Brough
They went down the Shafts, early each Morn
They did not bother, to shave
But took on their Backs, powder and Horn
To blow out, the lead from its Grave
The people of Bradwell, lead mined for Years
But now, they have closed them down

In the Journal of the Derbyshire Archaeological Society, 1911, Seth Evans wrote of

". . . lead mining in all the district surrounding Bradwell, where the industry was carried on by the Romans. Until the decline of the industry (circa 1880), most of the inhabitants of Bradwell - women and children as well as men - were employed at the mines, which run from east to west for a distance of four miles, in fact the whole parish is undermined, in some instances houses being built over the shaft of the mine."

An excellent book on the "Industrial Archaeology of the Peak District" by Helen Harris contains details of the history of lead mining in and around Bradwell. Cheet's reference to clean lead being handed down to Brough is borne out by the fact that this was the location of Brough White Lead Works where lead smelting was conducted from the middle of the eighteenth century. The terrible dangers associated with the lead industry are illustrated in an account in Helen Harris's book. On 18 April 1854 at the Slag Works, one of four cupolas sited in Bradwell, four people were suffocated to death by poisonous fumes arising from a fault in the pump engine.

WHEN YOU'RE FEELING NAZZY

When you're moody and you're Snappy
or your Head is full of pain
And your Stomach's feeling pappy
Or you've got a little Strain
{Just think of all the times you had}
{When you were well and Strong.}

If you've got a Cough & Sneezing
Or Rheumatics in your Knee
And your Chest is Slightly Wheezing
Or your Stick is never Free
{Just think of all the Times you had}
{When you were well and Free.}

When your back is very Naughty
Or your Feet not full of pep
And you're Thirty, over Forty
Or you Sometimes miss a Step
{Just think of all the Times you had}
{In your young Courting days.}

When you're Nazzy with your Missus
Or your Daughter likes a Smoke
And you catch her giving Kisses
Just treat it as a Joke
{And think of all the times you had}
{in your young Manhood days.}

When your Shoulders feel as Broken
Just keep it to Yourself
And you will get a Token
From off the Golden Shelf.

A FEW LINES ABOUT THE WINTER IN JAN AND FEB 1940, by C W Fletcher

I've heard, the old Folks, Talk a lot
Of Winters, in bygone days
But I don't want, to make a Blot
Or Cross them, with their Nays
When we have had, a lot of Snow
And when, we've been fed up
The old folks say, you do not Know
What Winters are, now sup.
While you are Supping, they Romance
And Talk, of days gone by.
They Wave their Arms, they Dance, They prance
Their Tales, they make you Sigh
Twas January, Nineteen Forty
the snow, fell very Deep
And things, my word, got very Haughty
Enough, to make you Weep
The Coal was Short, the Taps they Froze
And buried were the Sheep.
No Bread had we, nor Yeast to Bake
And things, looked very Black
Our Meat was short, and so was Steak
Through Snow, we could not Hack
The Trains were Stuck, The roads were Blocked
With Drifts, & Blocks of Ice

*Motor Engines, were all locked
As fingers, in a Vice
The Lights went out, for Hours on end
The Schools, they were, closed down
And folks, they had no way to fend
To find, their way down Town.*

*The Days were Cold, the Nights were Dark
Because of the Blackout
The Folks, that Stood, were nearly Stark
They could not get about
Icicles hung from every Spout
From Eaves Close to the Floor
Some were thin, & some were Stout
And some, Broad as a Door
Drifts were Twenty, & Thirty, feet High
Fowls cotes, were Buried for days
And the people of Bradwell, had little to Fry
No Food, did come their Ways
It Stopped the Milkmen, bringing Milk
The Fowls, they did not lay
You Saw, no ladies, dressed in Silk
No doubt, it did not pay.
And when at last the thaw set in
It found the Leaks and Flaws
It dropped off roofs with such a din
Like Men with Giant rip saws.*

It fetched the Spouts off, by the yard
And pipes, began to leak
It made things very, very, Hard
For people, in the Peak
What made it worse, the War was on
And Ration Books, in go
But now, we're Glad, the Snow has Gone
Although it has been Slow.

A FEW LINES ABOUT COLIN FLETCHER'S LODGER WHO GOT DRUNK AND LOST AND WENT AND KNOCKED MR FISCHER UP IN THE MIDDLE OF THE NIGHT IN FEBRUARY 1940 WHILE THE STORM WAS ON:

The snow lay on the Ground, in Drifts
And everywhere, 'Twas Dark
A man who'd been , to Earls on Shifts
Got drunk, and lost his Mark.
The Man whose name, we'll say was Tim
Did like, a glass of Beer
It seemed to give, poor Tim some Vim
And then, he had no Fear.
Now this Man, he lodged at Colins
Who lived, near Bethlehem Church
Did one night start, to make his Dins
When he, was in the Lurch.
At Knowles's pub, he had his Drink
Then Home, he thought he'd Go

But Tim, he did not stop to Think
And past, his Lodge did Blow.
He got right down, to Harvey's Yard
Then Knocked, at Fischer's Door
The light was out, the door was Barred
And Fischer, was very Sore.
Now Mr Fischer, was in Bed
But Tim, did Knock, Knock, Knock
I'm sure that Tim, had lost his Head
Or he, was off his Block.
Fischer lit, his Bit of Candle
And came, downstairs, ill Clad
And when, he'd undone the door Handle
Poor Tim, looked very Sad.
Now take me Home, please take me Home
Said Tim, please take my Hand
For I don't Know, how I did Roam
So far, from my Home Land.
Poor old Fischer, in Slippers and Socks
Turned out, in the Cold Cold Snow
I bet he wished, old Tim in the Stocks
As the Icy wind, did Blow.
When They arrived, at Colin's Gate
Tim said, he'd never Forget
He called poor Fischer, a jolly good Mate
He'd never, be out of his Debt.
Fischer said, no, never Shall I
But see, you don't do it again
For now I must bid, you just Goodbye
As this, has give me a pain.

JOKES FROM BRADWELL
by Cheetham William Fletcher

A lad went & got a job with a farmer. He hadent been long when an old Cow died. They had it for dinners untill it was finished. Then the old sow died: that went the same way. Then the old woman died, so the Farmers boy packed up. He wasent having old woman for dinner.

Jabez worked at Brough Lead Works. One day he was working away when the Boss came up to him & said very small shovel you've got Jabez. Yes says Jabez, Small Wage, Small Shovel.

The Sexton was digging a Grave in Bradwell Church Yard when up comes a Howling Tough. My word say's he, I dont suppose the people die very often round here. No Sir says the Sexton, Only Once.

Bobby Brown, who was the Policeman before the 1914 War, was one night running after some Lads accross a field at night time, when he thought he had got one who was laid under the Wall. By doe Ive got you dis time says Bobby Brown laying on with his stick. When he thought he had done enough & came to put his light on, it was a dead Sheep he had been hitting.

One Xmas time a Bradwell Man had been cutting thick Branches off a Tree near Hungry Lane. He was watched by another man who at night time went and fetched the branches and cut them into logs. Next day the man who cut the branches went to the other mans house telling him what he would do if he could find out who it was who had pinched his branches as he stood warming his back to the fire that had his own logs burning.

Bobby Brown was taking a youth to Castleton Lock up. On the way the youths hat blew over the wall. Can I fetch my hat says the youth. Yes says Bobby Brown. Of course the lad ran away. Next day, Bobby Brown was taking him to Castleton again, when the lads hat went off again. Can I fetch my hat Mr. Brown. No says he you ran away yesterday. You stay here I'll fetch it for you.

Two Bradwell Lads went to Sheffield on their first visit. After a while they got hungry and thought they would go and have some food. When they got inside & having a first course the Waitress came up & said Would you two young men like a serviette. Yes says one I think I could eat one if my pal can. The same two lads went to the pictures after having had their feed. When they got sat down one says they are funny seats these. He was sat on the seat top, with his feet on the seat.

When the Dore & Chinley line was first opened one train was just going in the tunnel and another one was just coming out when a Bradwell man said by Gum mate that was a bit of Good Steering wasent it

1938

Billy Revell was coming from off Abney Moor after pumping (it was very dry Weather). He saw a pool of Water in the road & he thought a water pipe had Bursted. He came down & fetched Mr. Shirt to have a look. Mr. Shirt was Chairman to the Council. They put the Listener on the spot & they where just going to fetch a man to dig down to the pipe, when an old Lady came out & said What are you looking for, because that Water is what Mr. David Bramalls Horse has done (It had made water).

Dr. McEntee of Bradwell Visited one of his patients & he told her to have a spoonfull of Whiskey at nights before going to bed. Doctor, says she, I have never had a drop of Whiskey in my life & I'm not starting now. The Doctor went home & mixed Whiskey & Water & put it in a Medicine Bottle & sent it to her. She wasent long before she sent the empty Bottle back, & would he send her another Bottle of the same sort, as it had done her so much good

Bobby O Who lived on the hills pulled one of those big purses out of his pocket & was taking some Money out. One of his old cronies said its a Deep purse you've got Bob. Ha he says, its deeper now than its ever been, One time I hadent to go as deep.

Beat lived in Smithy Hill. One day she said to her friend By Gum my feet do Hesitate me, she meant her Feet Irritated her.

Sam Middleton saw his little girl playing in the Brook. Go home says Sam if that not Home when I get Home I shall give you some Belt (He would have had a job if she wasent there).

I heard a good tale re the Air Raids & Mr. & Mrs. George Elliott, who live at Little Hucklow. Hucklow school Children Called & told them there was an Air Raid on at Bradwell. There wasent of course. George & his Wife sat all night with their Gas Masks on.

Big Gud, George Elliott who lives in Bradwell, went to Hucklow & he got drunk, he fell coming down Bradwell Dale & someone found him. Leave me alone says Gud Im unconsous.

TALES OF BRADWELL & ROUNDABOUT

When the Dore & Chinley line first opened A Bradwell man went to catch the Train down to Sheffield. Just as he got to the Station the Train was puffing out & of Course he missed it. Ha he says, if you go off like that without waiting for people, you will soon loose your Customers.
Ha said a Bradwell man who worked at Hadfields at Pindale, Said he to the Boss, a Horse & cart's rolled down the Tip & Their Both Killed.

Who was it that put the pig on the wall to hear the Band play? Who sawd the cows head off when it got its head fast in the Gate Bars? Who dug a hole & then found he had too much soil then he dug another hole to put the Spare soil in? Who put the Candles in the oven to dry? Who pulled the Cow up the

Steeple to eat the Grass? Who put wire netting round the Garden to keep the Cuckoo in? Who was it? went to Little Hucklow, had a drink too many, then when he was coming down Bradwell dale he said he had seen a big Black Bear, (a prank)
Who was found in Larry road drunk when he was found, he said leave me alone I'm unconscious?

(One of the Evacuees staying in Bradwell) His parents wanted him to go home to Chorlton for Xmas, so he said to the people who he was staying with in Bradwell, I hope old Hitler comes over & Bombs Chorlton just before Xmas. Then I shall not have to go home shall I.

Mrs. Rachel Hall who lived up Far Hill went to Sheffield by Car. Coming back at Night, she noticed the red discs in the Curbs, The danger Signals to Motorists. Ha she said to the Driver, do they keep those lights on all night & day, or do they turn them out in the day time?

Chapter 6
The Last Few Months

Two poems from Joyce's Autograph Book:

Joy was a Girl, who was in Camp
Roy was a Boy, Just her Stamp
They made it up, beneath a Lamp
To get Married, and save their stamps

The Weddings arranged, for August First
Things are likely, to go with a Burst
Joy seems windy, but Roy is Worse
Its not so long, since both were Nursed

We wish them Happy all through Life
Joy will make a D**n good Wife
If through life, they both will Strive
They are matched, so they will Thrive

We wish them Joy, and Happiness
good things in Life, we wish them Best
When they Come back, to Build a Nest
I think, they will, have earned a Rest.

C W Fletcher
Antique Dealer
Bradda
July 13th, 1942

When Joy comes Home to Bradda Town
To Settle down in Life
I shall, have gained, another Crown
As Roy, will Have a Wife

They Both, are Matched, as you can See
A Daughter, I shall Gain
And Roy, my Son, will Happy Be
They will, be like a Chain.

Grace Fletcher
Bradwell
July 13th, 1942

Cheet's daughter-in-law Joyce, from her home in North Wales, was able to provide some clear memories of Cheet' from the period 1942-1943.

Recalling her first meeting with Cheet' . . . "Roy and I were on weekend leave, just a Saturday night really, and Cheet' and Grace took us to the Bowling Green. That same weekend he took us to his parents' home and also to see Colin and Alice at their home in Hugh Lane, opposite the first chapel, and also to see Jack and Betty at Dialstones". She went on to say "I was in the WRNS and only visited Bradwell on weekend leaves. We married in August 1942 and had just one night at Bradwell because Roy's leave had been rearranged at the last minute from 2 weeks to 2 days. On April 1st 1943 I came out of the WRNS because I was pregnant. I didn't know many people in Bradwell, apart from a few relatives. Cheet' was very kind and would take me walking and as we returned he'd take me to visit other people in the village."

Roy and Joyce's Wedding Day; 1 August 1942. Back row from left to right: Len Bridgen (Joyce's father), Grace, Roy, Joyce, Eddie Roberts (best man), Florence (Joyce's mother), Cheet', John Fletcher and Betty (Jack's wife). Foreground: Nancy (Joyce's WRNS friend), Len (Joyce's brother) and Muriel (Joyce's sister).

Another memory related to Cheet' getting smartly dressed for funerals for which he would wear long coat and top hat. She didn't know about this, having been used to seeing Cheet' dressed in short sleeves or overalls most of the time. One day she became aware of this finely dressed old guy tipping his top hat and winking at her from the other side of the road which caused her to go into the house and express her indignation about the cheeky so-and-so . . . only to be told by Grace "it's Cheet', he's doing a funeral for Jack".

Roy and Joyce on their wedding day

Len and Florence together with Grace and Cheet' on Roy and Joyce's wedding day. Florence died in 1953. Len and Grace were married in 1956 and enjoyed five years of happiness together.

Joyce told how one day Cheet' had asked her to help him play a trick on an old guy who was well known for scrounging tobacco. She was asked to engage the man in conversation and whilst he was distracted Cheet' would offer him some dark twist contaminated with strips of rubber. The man apparently took the tobacco, smoked it, and never knew the difference!

Cheet' once invited Joyce on an outing with him to Bakewell which she gladly accepted. Later she was quite shocked to discover that they were travelling with the hearse driver to collect the body of a young woman who had died in childbirth.

Joyce gave birth to Barry Fletcher on 21 September 1943 and she described Cheet's happiness on becoming a grandfather. Roy was unable to get leave of absence and Cheet' was delighted to take a major role at the Christening in St Barnabas Church.

The following month Cheet' was working nights at the Newburgh engineering works on Netherside, Bradwell where he was engaged on war-related work. He went to bed during the morning of 31 October 1943 and when Grace went to him later in the day she could not waken him. He had passed away peacefully in his sleep.

From the Sheffield Star of Tuesday 2 November, 1943 under Deaths:

"FLETCHER, Cheetham W, suddenly at his home, Townend, Bradwell, Oct. 31st. Interment, Bradwell Church, on Thursday Nov 4th at 2.30 pm. Friends please accept this, the only invitation."

Barry Fletcher remembered his grandmother Grace telling him that Cheet' had died of a 'fatty heart'. Joyce Fletcher said that Cheet' died of 'an enlarged heart'. His death certificate confirms cause of death as "coronary occlusion - fatty degeneration of heart".

Cheet's Funeral was held on 4 November 1943. He had said to Grace that if he was to die first he did not want his funeral to be 'a morbid do with everyone crying and miserable'. He would like the Memorial Hall thrown open for anyone to attend. Thus there was no 'bidding' in the form of persons going round to friends and acquaintances informing them of funeral details and confirming their invitation.

As it was rationing time there was need for much improvisation. Joyce went in Jack's car, with Aunt Alice, to Bakewell, early in the morning on the day of the funeral. Their purpose was to purchase all fresh cakes, pastries and bread that they could find and to bring these back to Bradwell. Lots of people were involved in the preparation, including Aunt Betty and Aunt Polly.

The church was overflowing and many, many people attended a fine tea in the Memorial Hall. Cheet's son Roy was allowed compassionate leave from the Navy to attend the funeral.

Cheet's grave is in St Barnabas church cemetery and bears the inscription:

> "To his gay and gallant spirit a happiness
> which once has been is imperishable".

CHAPTER 7
REFLECTIONS BY BILL FLETCHER

From the moment my brother, Barry, first approached me about putting together a book on our grandfather, Cheetham William Fletcher, I felt it had to happen. Why? Well there were several reasons.

As a youngster I had always felt I had missed out on grandparents; by the age of eleven all had died. Of all my grandparents people seemed mostly to talk about Cheet', he seemed to have left his mark, people had lots of fond memories. In my early years I used to help tend his grave with my father and I often returned on my own to talk to Cheet' and tell him what was happening in my life. I felt I knew him yet he died seven years before I was born.

I wanted this book to happen so that Cheet' would live on, so others would get an insight into his life and get to know him a little bit. I had read Cheet's journal several times and the thought of others being able to share the journal felt right.

Finally and probably my main reason, to have achieved something with my brother. Brothers can be all sorts of different things: mine has been someone who cares and he has always been there for me and supported me in many ways during my life. To see in print something put together by the two of us would seem the culmination of the work that has gone into strengthening our relationship over the past few years. Throughout the years I have always been proud of my brother and feel that to see my name alongside his on a publication about our grandfather would be a very proud moment for me.

When we had not long been researching the idea, I realised how little I actually knew about my grandfather. Together we realised we knew when he died, but not when he was born, where he was born, where he had lived, in fact the list seemed quite endless. Gradually the answers started to arrive; copy birth certificate, copy marriage certificate, photographs, letters, post cards, and the picture began to build. Every phone call between Barry and myself seemed to bring some new discovery; something or someone in Cheet's journal was identified; from somewhere a bit more information; another piece of the jigsaw.

I started to look at our grandfather's journey through World War I. We had the information in the journal which left me in no doubt about the trauma experienced and the horror seen. What it did not do for me was to make me stop and think what could be learned from the information and what could we find out by the expansion of the notes. At first I started to track the final year (1918), using maps and information from reference books and whilst a route soon became apparent this was not enough.

I wanted to try and imagine what it must have been like, to empathise with my granddad. My needs were triggered by the Regimental Historian of the Sherwood Foresters who provided information about some members of the regiment, mentioned in Cheet's journal, who had been killed in action and in particular Sergeant George H Holmes. On the computer printout, in the section "buried/commemerated" were the words "no known grave". Cheet's journal for 25 September 1918 states "George Holmes another pal got killed". Cheet' knew his friend had died yet there was no body to bury: only the words "another pal got killed". I stopped and opened my mind.

Cheetham William Fletcher was twenty years old when he ran away from home to join the army on 7 September 1914. Five months later Cheet' landed in France. I think of a young man of twenty years who had lived most of his life in a village; a man to whom most places were visited on foot; a man to whom a visit to Sheffield (approximately fifteen miles) must have seemed an excursion; a man who suddenly finds himself hundreds of miles from home in the middle of a war. The main aim survival: not just for one day, one week, one month but for four years.

There must have been times when it seemed it would go on forever. Fighting for loved ones back home, fighting for what you thought was right. I have often tried to think what it must have been like, day after day, being thrown together in new friendships, then being there when they were killed, putting that behind you and getting on with the next day. All I can feel is that no matter what my personal feelings, necessity or waste, I feel humbled by the memory of people like our granddad and I also start to feel some of the pain.

When I moved on to look at Cheet's involvement with the Home Guard, I looked at the notes in a totally different way to any I had before. I was aware of, and had watched many times, the television programme 'Dads Army' which "sends up" the Home Guard but can now no longer look at it in the same way. I do not feel the programme projects how people like our grandfather must have looked at what was happening. They had fought in "the War to end Wars"; they had experienced first hand the horrors and to them the second war was very real. To them the invasion could happen at any time and once again they were willing to fight for their loved ones. There must have been a rekindling of all the memories: twenty-one years to try and put it all behind you, but now the memories return. Where they had once been waved off by their parents, now they in turn waved off their sons. I cannot possibly conceive what it must have meant to them.

I wonder now if it all became too much for Cheet'. I wonder if this is why he went to sleep on 31 October 1943 and did not wake up again.

To me the book is many things. It reminds me of Cheet': in many ways it has brought me nearer to him and this in turn has increased my love for him. It has made me appreciate what is around me, the loved ones and friends old and not yet known. By not knowing Cheet', by missing the love of a grandfather, I am made more aware of the love I share with others. I shall always have the memories of how excited Barry has become on finding out just that little bit more information. I envy him his enthusiasm. I thank the book for bringing us closer together: there have been many enjoyable conversations around getting to know our granddad.

It has reminded me of friends and relatives gone from this earth and what they gave me in life. These memories have been both pain and joy and show how both the past and present have made me who I am.

I hope that people reading this book will enjoy it both "as a read" and as a reminder of those brave men who risked everything for us today. I would also hope that, as it has for me, it makes the reader appreciate those around them and brings them a little closer together.

William Cheetham Fletcher

23 September 1997

CHAPTER 8
REFLECTIONS ON THE WRITING OF THIS BOOK

I started typing Cheet's journal into computer on 6 January 1995. At that time it was a way of safeguarding his writing and making it easier to save and copy. It wasn't until early 1997 that the idea of using his work in a book came to me. The remainder of this chapter, based on my notes, describes some of the thoughts and feelings which have been uncovered during the journey of writing this book.

18 February 1997; Derbyshire Records' Office (DRO), Matlock:
An informative article in the 'Peak Advertiser' had described the work of the DRO and alerted me to the possibility of learning about Cheet's ancestors. I can still feel the sheer excitement of discovering the name 'Fletcher' on a fragment of 1729 Peak Forest Parish record whilst sat at one of the DRO's film viewers. I carefully wrote down the page number and location and moved on to scan further baptism records. James, to Francis and Mary; Mary, to Henry and Elizabeth; Edward, to Henry and Elizabeth; Elizabeth, to John and Joan; Martha, to John and Joan; John, to Henry and Elizabeth; Mary, to Francis and Mary. These added up to seven baptisms in the six years ending 1734.

Undeterred I persisted with my task, recording key details as I moved through the decades and eventually to the 1780s. At the end of several hours work I took stock: 63 baptisms of children born to 16 different couples named Fletcher in the period 1729 to 1786. This was a powerful piece of learning and showed the enormity, and possible futility, of trying to trace a family by starting at the wrong end - that is oldest rather than youngest first.

On the same day I came across a family tree for a particular line of Fletchers of Peak Forest which had been prepared by James Dunn of Hyde, Cheshire. His work contained a note that "A truly comprehensive tree of Peak Forest Fletchers would require a paper as big as Pedlicote Farm and perhaps bigger".

Journeying from the records' office I decided on the importance of meeting up with relatives where contact had been minimal or even nil. Later that week I called to see Cheet's nephew Noel. I can remember the excitement expressed by Noel when I gave to him extracts from Cheet's journal relating to the Home Guard. Looking back I realise this was a starting point for me to jot down stories and memories that others have: separating out their real memories from their stories and the stories passed to them.

25 February 1997; Hinckley Island Hotel, Leicestershire:
A quick meeting with brother Bill and his wife Jackie to talk through the project and to identify some of what we were getting ourselves into. Bill brought a brown paper bag containing old papers, Cheet's war medals, maps and other memorabilia.

27 April 1997:
Bill and Jackie came to Sunday lunch and for us to review progress. I could tell that Bill was really coming on stream: he walked up our path weighted down with bulging carrier bags which when opened revealed numerous books about WW1. I warmed to the prospect of our working together on the project, the sense of togetherness and jointly facing the challenge. I sensed our becoming closer and a realisation that until this project our only joint working was to tend the family graves once a year. With this project we would be deeply involved in keeping each other up to date; in gathering information; in taking decisions; in wanting to share with each other the thrill of new discoveries.

16 May 1997:
Through the post I receive copies of Cheet's birth and marriage certificates from Marian Smith at Bakewell Register Office. These are most welcome and give me a feeling of being on an important journey.

23 May 1997:
Great joy in calling to see my Aunt May in Bradwell; my oldest surviving relative (born 1909). We took great pleasure in racking our brains and jotting down memories which she recalled from countless conversations with her second husband Jack, Cheet's brother. May made a quick telephone call and in less than an hour we arrived at Dam Dale Farm, Peak Forest. May's last visit had been 9 years earlier around the time of Jack's death. On this my first visit I was delighted to meet Ned and Sheila Fletcher and quickly realised how interested she was in family history. Seeing their family tree was a delight, especially seeing the links and overlaps with my own and being able to fill some important gaps. I was close to tears on being shown the Last Will & Testament of John Fletcher who was my great great great grandfather.

6 June 1997:
Why is it only now, spurred on to write this book, that I feel such sadness for things undone? Initial sadness that I could have found out so much more about my grandfather from his brothers and my father. I could have asked them and they would have been pleased and delighted to tell their stories - enriched by their perceptions, their memories and the things that were important to them. All we would have needed was a quiet space, some time and my opening question "What do you remember about my grandfather?" With good ears and a quickness of note taking I could have captured hundreds of pearls: stories and recollections which are now lost forever. How wasteful and careless of me not to have tapped into these sources of rich information.

But my sadness goes deeper than this; much deeper. I now realise something much more important about the nature of 'family'. To have encouraged my father and great-uncles to talk about my grandfather would have been to engage with them. To jointly travel a journey on which our common ground was my grandfather: their knowledge and experiences combining with my need to find out, resulting in a deep and real sharing between us.

June 1997:
Heightened feelings from seeing the television programme documentary on General Sir Douglas Haig and realising Cheet' was there and how lucky he was to return - something like 750,000 troops had been killed in Haig's army. Also, making the connection that Cheet' had been in the same vicinity as Wilfred Owen - about 3 days difference in position when Owen was killed. I have been greatly moved by Owen's writing and influenced by Dominic Hibberd's book. Referring to the war in France during September 1918 Hibberd speaks of newspapers being full of praise for the latest successes. He goes on to say "The men who had done the fighting were less forthcoming, knowing what it meant to kill and see one's friends killed; they had survived by chance, and they remembered comrades who had not". Quoting from Owen's 'Spring Offensive':

> And crawling slowly back, have by degrees
> Regained cool peaceful air in wonder -
> Why speak not they of comrades that went under?

Hibberd suggests that Owen wanted the poem to be understood by soldiers; only they would see the point of his final question.

5 July 1997:

LOSS

What did Cheet' feel on being in France?
He doesn't say
But in his own blunt way
He speaks of good friends killed
and snatched away.

WAR

In the trenches
seeing his friends
gassed, wounded and killed.
Digging their graves
fashioning their crosses
with each passing hour, wondering
if his time would come.
And then the bullet in his chest
Christmas nineteen fifteen
wounded in action.
Return to England
recuperation
marriage
then back to France
to fight for two more years
and more.

18 July 1997, Sunset (reflecting on an earlier visit):
I travelled up to Bradwell to see the War Memorial in St Barnabas's Church yard - perhaps I could make some connections between the names that Cheet' had mentioned and those who had died in the First World War. I wrote down the 33 names of Bradwell men killed in that war and the 6 killed in the Second World War. I noticed one of the names 'L E A Middleton' and wondered if this was the Lionel Middleton who Cheet' enlisted with. A sombre few minutes thinking how easily Cheet's name could have been on the list and also reflecting how life might have been for those in France and also for their families and friends left in Bradwell.

I was also struck by the number of people who had lost their lives, especially in the first war. These 33 men must have been a significant proportion of the young men from the village and there can be little doubt that everyone in Bradwell would have been affected in some way by their deaths. A thought came into my mind that the premature demise of these young men determined that they did not go on to become fathers and grandfathers. This reduced the numbers of young children who might have gone to Bradwell schools in the 1940s, some of whom would have become my school friends.

As I walked away from the War Memorial I heard the unmistakable noise of many children at play - a noise which drew me to the gates of the school which had been attended by me in the 1940s and by Roy my father in the 1920s. I was wondering if Cheet' had been at the same school around the end of the nineteenth century. A number of young children saw me struggling to open the gate to the school yard. They showed me how it opened and as I walked into the yard three or four of them clung onto me, pulling me around and swinging playfully on my arms. Suddenly I was transported back in time almost 50 years to my childhood as a pupil, at playtime in that familiar school yard. In a corner, adjoining the drive up to the school, is a large cube of sandstone and I was reminded, so clearly, that this had served as a castle, a prison and a vantage point during my many hours of play in that school.

21 July 1997:

MYSTERY

When you penned these words
did you ever think
that 60 years later
your grandson would read your stories
of childhood, village life and two world wars
and be moved to tears
of joy and sorrow?

GRANDSON

On the birth of your grandson
what did you feel?
I'd like to think you were overjoyed
despite the fact that within six short weeks
your life would end.

25 July 1997:
Closing my eyes; focusing my brain; concentrating on my grandfather Cheetham William Fletcher. Words inside my head tell me this is fruitless . . "you never knew him, so how can you remember him?" I persevere in the knowledge that he knew me and therefore it may be possible for me to remember him. I have no memories, proper memories that is, where I can visualise myself and Cheet in the same place and see our surroundings and hear his voice and be there again. After all I wasn't yet six weeks' of age when he died on 31 October 1943 so maybe I am expecting too much when I strive to remember situations which we both shared.

When I concentrate on his two brothers, Colin and Jack, I have real memories. For example, on saying their names I fleetingly see their faces in my mind's eye; I remember seeing them and hearing their voices. I remember calling to see Colin and Alice and granny Fletcher (Annie) at Hills View.

Annie as I remember her

Colin worked on Earl's, often wore overalls and seldom was without his flat cap. There were Christmas visits to each other's houses, usually ending in some games of cards for halfpennies and pennies plus food galore. Further memories of Colin pulling Alice's leg whilst playing cards - she had a way of speaking emphatically when the cards were going her way and Colin would reflect her words back to her. Another tale of Colin losing his teeth one night and sending son Brian out to find them, successfully. Colin had a small motor-bike for going to work, a BSA Bantam I think, which was overshadowed by the powerful bikes that Brian used to own. Colin reared pigs and I can recall one awful memory of a squealing pig being slaughtered. Later he kept chickens and often would give away the eggs.

I remember walking up to Jack and Betty's house at Dialstones in the 1950s. On their sideboard an ornate brass clock with rotating parts; their talk of their lost son, George. Jack and Noel popping across to our house from their workshop at Townend; me wandering across and watching them at work. Jack's sheer delight in working with wood and showing me how the tools do the work. A place for each of his tools. And the machinery, his watchful eye making sure I didn't stray into danger. The way he cherished successive Morris Travellers with careful attention to woodwork repairs and varnishing. His indignation when other road users would blow their horns because everyone should know that he always reversed out of the joiners' shop yard. The care he took, rotating the wood stock; stacking, unstacking, restacking.

The sad loss of his wife Betty in 1960 on top of all his earlier losses. And then his new bride of 1964, my great Aunt May, seeing them happy and bubbling with life. Calling to see them, still at Dialstones; the chair-lift as he became more frail. His stories of undertaking, blowing-up the floor of the cottage, moving home only a few yards in the whole of his life. And then, later, when he had stopped work, a dear old man in his nineties, I remember his chair, his smile on seeing me. His smoking by taking a few draws on a cigarette and then with small scissors cutting off the burning end and allowing it to drop into an ashtray, the remainder being put aside for later. I remember his body warmers and peaked hats. I cherish the treasured gift from Aunt May of Jack's walking stick with the bone handle and silver ferrule.

GRIEF

How did Jack feel to lose his father
and then his elder brother
and then his son George
killed at Arnhem
so close to what was to be
the end of the war?
How can a man cope with the loss
of father, brother and son
in the short space
of fourteen months?
So many losses.
What did he feel?

There are no such memories which I can recall for granddad Cheet'. The picture which does come to mind is a head and shoulders portrait of him which hangs on my office wall. I'm looking at that picture now and remembering that it wasn't always on my wall. There are several copies and as a young boy of four or five I can remember my grandmother, Grace or Nanan as I knew her, showing me that same picture and talking to me about Cheet', her lost husband. She used to live next door to us at Townend, Bradwell. She had the adjoining cottage and I used to visit her often: at that time she was my only accessible grandparent because my mum's parents lived in Staffordshire. She used to tell me about my grandfather and shared with me some of her sadness and her memories.

In her living room my grandmother had a bureau with a hinged lid which, when opened, rested on two sliding supports. I can see that bureau now, with the lid open and the two of us sat in front of it. She used to show me some of the contents of the small drawers, objects which had belonged to Cheet'. I can see two tin whistles and a tiny replica of a pistol which was a mere inch or so in length. I used to be drawn to this little pistol - I have it now and can only assume that she gave it to me. With pride she would show me the framed certificate commemorating the fact that Cheet' had been mentioned in despatches. Thinking about those times now I can begin to see how sad she must have been to have lost her husband before he reached the age of 50.

St Annes on Sea with Nanan; circa 1949

26 July 1997:
Whilst out walking with Joan and our dog Zoe we met Jack Bough and I spent a short while talking to him. Yes he did remember his uncle Cheet' and it began to dawn on me that he was not alone in remembering my grandfather. Something new he told me was that he and his family had lived with Cheet' and Grace for a few weeks during the 1930s. We agreed I would give Jack a call and arrange to meet to discuss in more detail.

29 July 1997:
At my mother's home in North Wales, searching through old papers and photographs, three treasures came to light. One a postcard sent by Grace to Cheet' on 18 September 1915, some three months before he would be wounded. Another, a photograph of 7 young men including 4 of those whom Cheet' wrote about in his 'drinking poem'. Last, and not least, the entry in Joyce's Autograph book: two poems written by Cheet', approximately three weeks before Roy and Joyce were married. This was such a find because it was something unexpected; poems that Cheet' had written outside his journal. In one of these he describes some feelings stemming from the imminent marriage and his gaining a daughter:

"... I shall have gained another Crown ... "

"... and Roy my Son will Happy be .. "

Also, relaxing in her sitting room after a good meal at the local hostelry, my mother was able to recall experiences and information which were new to me and which helped to fill some of the gaps in my knowledge. Before returning home I asked my mother if she would look for photographs of Grace and her family, write down any memories of Grace and send these to me.

6 August 1997:

I spent two full hours looking through Eric Gill's magnificent collection of photographs of Bradwell throughout the ages. These are often displayed in the Methodist Chapel during the week of Bradwell Wakes and Well Dressing. I was intrigued by the detail to which Eric had gone in identifying people, places and dates - I made a few notes of facts which would prove helpful in filling some of my gaps in knowledge. Unfortunately Eric did not appear to like me doing this - such a shame because I have no intention of upstaging him, as if I could! Also, my finished work will be made available to him and act as a useful supplement to his vast array of information on local history.

Later that day, sitting in Wilf and Dorothy Cushworth's front room, I read some of Cheet's writing to Wilf. One particular poem about some Bradwell lads going drinking touched a chord and his face creased in laughter and recollection. As names were mentioned he filled in details or coaxed his brain to remember some fragment of the past.

8 August 1997:

Friday, a very hot, sunny day and during the afternoon I rang Jack Bough to see if it was convenient to call. Around 3.30 I sat with Jack and his wife Helen in their house at Mytham Bridge, Bamford. Jack was able to recall lots of memories, especially of the mid 1930s and the hardship they experienced when his father Harry was out of work. At this meeting I decided to research more about Grace and her roots and family in order to achieve some balance. Jack provided some good information which filled a number of gaps and reminded me quite vividly of some of the times when I had gone with Nanan (Grace) to visit Aunt Emily and Uncle Harry at Winhill View on the Hope Road near the Rising Sun Hotel. I find it hard to accept that Grace and I used to travel from Townend Bradwell to Winhill View on roller skates!

Grace and her brother Harry outside Winhill View, Hope Road, Bamford; circa 1958

19 August 1997:
Through the post I received some photographs and some writing from my mother - these were specifically about my grandmother Grace. I was so pleased to receive them because in working with Cheet's material I had become so aware that he did not mention Grace at all in his journal. The seed of this realisation had been born on first reading.

This evening I rang mum to thank her for what she had sent. We chatted for quite a while and she was able to amplify what she had written and to provide further memories. Some while after we had finished she rang back to tell me that she had started to do some knitting after our conversation and that her mind was wandering into the past memories of Grace.

She had realised that memories were being triggered and that some of her previous information may not be completely accurate, so she rang to tell me this and to talk through the 'correct' version. What I like about this vignette is that she had moved from a position of being stuck, where she remembered little and found difficulty in writing down anything. Her memory had been 'triggered' by photographs and now she was able to write something, discuss it with me, amplify it, reflect more deeply and remember new things. There is something here about the capacity to 'recall' and 'recollect' which potentially is available to all or at least many of us.

25 August 1997:
Bank Holiday Monday I rang Bill Bough and within 30 minutes I was sat with him in his front room on Brentwood Road, Bamford. Whilst on the phone to him he'd said he doubted whether he could add any information to what his brother Jack had already provided. I found this idea interesting, especially as he didn't know what Jack had said. However he said he would like us to meet and when I arrived he was obviously so pleased to see me. We stood in his kitchen, shaking hands and looking at each other, I think to see some feature by which we could recognise the other person. Early on in our conversation he mentioned his son, also named Barry, and I need to record here that I had no picture in my mind's eye of this man until a few minutes later when a picture, so crystal clear and focused, came flooding into my head.

For maybe ten or fifteen minutes we chatted generally and then it was clear to me that Bill wanted to talk more deeply about the sad loss of his wife some 13 years earlier. I found myself thinking that had I not been researching for this book I would not have visited him and I would not have been sharing these precious feelings with him.

I'm reminded of George Parritt seeing me for the second time and leaning over towards me to say that he'd been thinking of our earlier conversation and that he realised he may have misled me. We talked through his 'new version' and he seemed really pleased to be putting the record straight. At one point he was in full flight and telling me about Briar Cottage when suddenly he came to an abrupt halt. He had forgotten the names of the people who lived there at the time of his story. I said it didn't matter but it completely blocked him, as if the brakes had been applied to his thought processes. We left it that he could let me know if the names came to him and I took my leave and set off up the hill to rejoin my brother. I'd been gone only a little while, a few minutes, when George came running, yes running, around the corner to tell me that he had remembered their name was Dungworth. This triggered further memory and the first names, Cissy and Ernest came to mind together with the fact that they were very close friends of Grace and Cheet'. He was so pleased to have remembered and this is another example of how memory can be triggered and revived.

27 August 1997:
I woke in the early hours and found myself unable to return to sleep which is very unusual for me. My brain is racing about this project and I hope this isn't going to be a regular occurrence. I so much want to get the book finished but realise I am in the dangerously open territory of containment; how and where do I draw the finishing or containing line for this book? If I am over cautious I'll never finish and I can anticipate that the detail produced will be too much for the average reader. I'm trying to accommodate so many threads and strands into the work, for example; photographs and other pictures, finding out about Cheet's school, planning a Bradwell walk with Bill, tight deadlines and not missing out anyone who knew Cheet' (a stupid objective because I don't even know who did know him and whether they are alive today). So where does this leave me? I think what I need to do is

to prepare yet another list but this time head it "actions which when completed will denote the end of the book". Having written this I feel lots better and energised for the task ahead.

Later that morning I was sat at my computer working on the book when the phone rang and it was Sheila from Dam Dale Farm at Peak Forest. I was so pleased that she was ringing me because I had written shortly after my first visit to meet her and Ned and I had heard nothing. We chatted and she confirmed I could reproduce the will in the book and that I could call anytime to see them. This felt good because until I'd started this project I had not known of their existence.

A few minutes after this call I rang Eric Gill in Bradwell to let him know how much I would value his help with some of the gaps in information. Also, how I would appreciate borrowing a few photographs of Cheet's haunts to put into the book. We chewed it over and I promised I would ensure that his contribution was fully acknowledged and he agreed to come along with me. This delighted me because he has a wealth of information and the book will be considerably enriched with his help.

In the afternoon I called to see Harry White, soon to be 88 years of age, who I had known in the past and who was mentioned in Cheet's writing about the Home Guard. When I rang him I had to briefly explain who I was and he made the connection when I mentioned my father Roy. He said over the phone that he doubted he would have much to contribute but we still agreed to meet around 3 pm. I called at his house, interestingly going straight to it from memory because I had called for his son Raymond at the same house some 35 years ago. Harry was in his garden and when I saw him I recognised him immediately, commenting that he had changed little. He said that other people made the same comment.

Seated in his house, Harry explained to me that he had moved to

Bradwell from Eyam in 1940. For a few years he lived in the adjoining house to Jack Fletcher's at Dialstones. It was important for him to tell me that his wife Annie had died in 1976 and that his sister, who stayed in the original house in Eyam, had died in 1996 aged 94 years. He was proud to tell me about his two sons and to bring me up to date with their lives and experiences. He was particularly proud of his grandson's academic achievements. Again I found myself being reminded that without the research for this book we would not have shared this important time together. We said our goodbyes and I set off for Brough Lea Farm, Bradwell.

How can I start to describe the excitement of going to Brian (Nat) and Pam's and trawling through so many treasures? Earlier Pam had said that she didn't think they would have much in the way of photographs and papers. I remember arriving home exhausted after spending nearly five hours at the farm - the longest time I'd ever spent with cousin Brian. This provides another example where researching the book provided the opportunity to spend time with a close relative; time which otherwise we would not have had. Nat and I had a shared quest revisiting our family's history; during that time together we talked of several important things, not least his recent poor health and how he felt about that.

I didn't realise it at the time but later I recognised how emotionally draining the experience had been. There we were, sorting through an old tin, with inner lid, in which had been stored dozens of old treasures: In Memoriam Cards, Postcards, photographs, bills, receipts and letters. I remember now the sad feelings on finding a black edged card "In Loving Memory of Sarah Annie Fletcher . . . who departed this life June 13th 1894 aged 2 years and 8 months". This had been Cheet's elder sister who I had not known about. I imagined the despair of losing Sarah Annie just six months after Cheet's birth.

I can still feel the excitement of discovering new pictures and information: of holding and studying embroidered cards which Cheet' had sent to his mother, father and brothers; the joy of opening the green envelope headed 'On Active Service' and taking out and unfolding the pencilled, three page letter Cheet' had sent to his mother from France in March 1917. And then being overwhelmed when Pam brought three more large tins of further photographs and correspondence, with our Nat saying we should sort through them all before putting them back.

28 August 1997:
Bill Bough rang with some further memories; this a man who had said he wouldn't be able to help. He commented on how little things were triggering his memory and how much he was enjoying the reminiscences. How good it felt to be in touch.

8 September 1997; Crovie, N Scotland:
In my endeavour to press on with the book about Cheet' I'm firmly focused onto clarifying the reasons for the book; the motivation to write it and to convert a bundle of passed-down memories, writings, pictures and other items into a tangible work.

Cheet' wrote his stuff in his way: why he wrote it may have few or many answers. Did he realise that one day his grandson, and within his knowledge his only grandson, would read his work so intently that he would wish to publish it for the world to see? Who has read Cheet's work? Certainly Grace will have pored over his journal in those lonely times after his untimely death. And how would she have felt about not being mentioned once by name? Also, Roy, Joyce and my brother Bill have read Cheet's work but I wonder if to the degree of detail, and with the same rigour, as me. So why the book? Just give a few good reasons why it should come to be.

Primarily I want his work to be noticed and known: not to be wasted. He invested a fair amount of energy in his writing and, not necessarily realising it, produced a work of history which to my knowledge is unique. Yes, others have made diaries and written accounts of their experiences but Cheet's work represents a full account of a lifetime. In 1937 when he started to write he couldn't have realised that his life would last for only six more years. There are some omissions; for example he does not mention Grace, his courtship, wedding nor birth of his son or grandson. This suggests he didn't reveal too much emotion. I have no doubt that he 'felt' the feelings of life but he did not express them.

Others' memories suggest that he would avoid expression of deep feeling through the diversion of a prank or joke. He would alleviate the sober occasion of a funeral with a wink to roadside onlookers and thus would lighten the moment. Another factor that has just come to mind is the extent to which he was exposed to close, personal loss or grief. Moving through his life he lost his sister Sarah Annie when he was 5 month's old, his sister Constance Ann died when he was 7 and his grandfather when Cheet' was 19. Who knows what losses he experienced during WW1? In his journal he speaks of several. Whilst in his 20s both of his wife's parents died. His dearly loved grandmother died in 1938 and his father John in 1943. There is little to show how these losses affected him although, for a man with a natural zest for life, the probable answer is severely.

18 September 1997:
I went to see Tom Buxton of Hope, a truly fine gentleman, who used to live on Church Street, Bradwell, opposite what is now the Valley Lodge, previously the new Shoulder of Mutton. Tom, born in 1904, came to Bradwell in February, 1935 where he stayed until 1948. As a soldier he had spent three years in the Grenadier Guards followed by nine years as a reserve. His time as a reserve

was within three weeks of finishing when war broke out in 1939. Needless to say he was called up immediately and instructed to report to Wellington Barracks near Buckingham Palace.

He recounted lots of stories to me and I could tell from his face that he was reliving the memories. Tom remembered Colin, Cheet's brother, with affection. Tom worked at the cement works driving dumper trucks and earth movers and one of Colin's duties involved helping in the canteen. One fond story involved Tom asking for a brew of tea to which Colin enquired "as t' brass?" or have you got the money? As a pensioner, Tom secured a part-time morning job in Bradwell helping out at a newsagents. This involved him in sorting out the papers into rounds and then delivering one of these himself. He recalled that he delivered the last newspaper in his round to Colin's at Hills View and that many times "Colin would have the fags and a mug of tea ready and we'd have a good chat".

18 October 1997; 0830, Saturday:
I'm sat at my computer feeling the heavy weight of an end of November deadline which I suggested and which has been agreed by Bob Mulholland of Peak Press. There is still unfinished business with the book: when I concentrate on what is still to be done I am almost overwhelmed! I have yet to obtain photographs of Dam Dale Farm and Cheet's grandfather; Eric Gill's treasure trove of pictures and information remains untapped; Eileen Knowles and Eileen Hancock's memories have not been rekindled; I'm still grappling with the title, long before the book is taking on its finished shape; my brother Bill's contribution is not yet fully known; there are pictures still to be dated and decisions taken on what to include or leave out; and so the list goes on.

What strikes me now, at this very moment, is why do I feel compelled to tie up so many loose ends to the point where I can say the job is finished? Life isn't really like that and usually there are jobs to be done and unfinished business. Cheet's journal was unfinished, as indeed were many other things that he probably wanted to do in his lifetime. So maybe I need to relax a bit, or 'chill out' to use a current expression. I need to give myself permission to accept that the researching and gathering of information will never be finished; even if the list above is met there will always be something more which I would like to have. This talk with myself has helped considerably to remove much of the pressure I was feeling. My conclusion now is that when the end of November arrives the book will be finished.

24 October 1997; 1000, Thornhill:

Whilst out walking with our dog Zoe, Joan and I witnessed a massive leaf fall following a very heavy frost the previous night and I am prompted to write:

SADNESS

Fixed spellbound
by the patter
of thousands
upon thousands
of falling leaves
prematurely
wrenched from life
reminded
of countless losses
in countless wars

30 November 1997; Hathersage:

MY GRANDFATHER

This man I never knew
this joker
this prankster
this man who went to war in France
this wounded soldier
this carpenter
this raconteur
this writer
this poet
this man who died too soon
this man I never knew.

Barry Fletcher

30 November 1997

APPENDIX 1

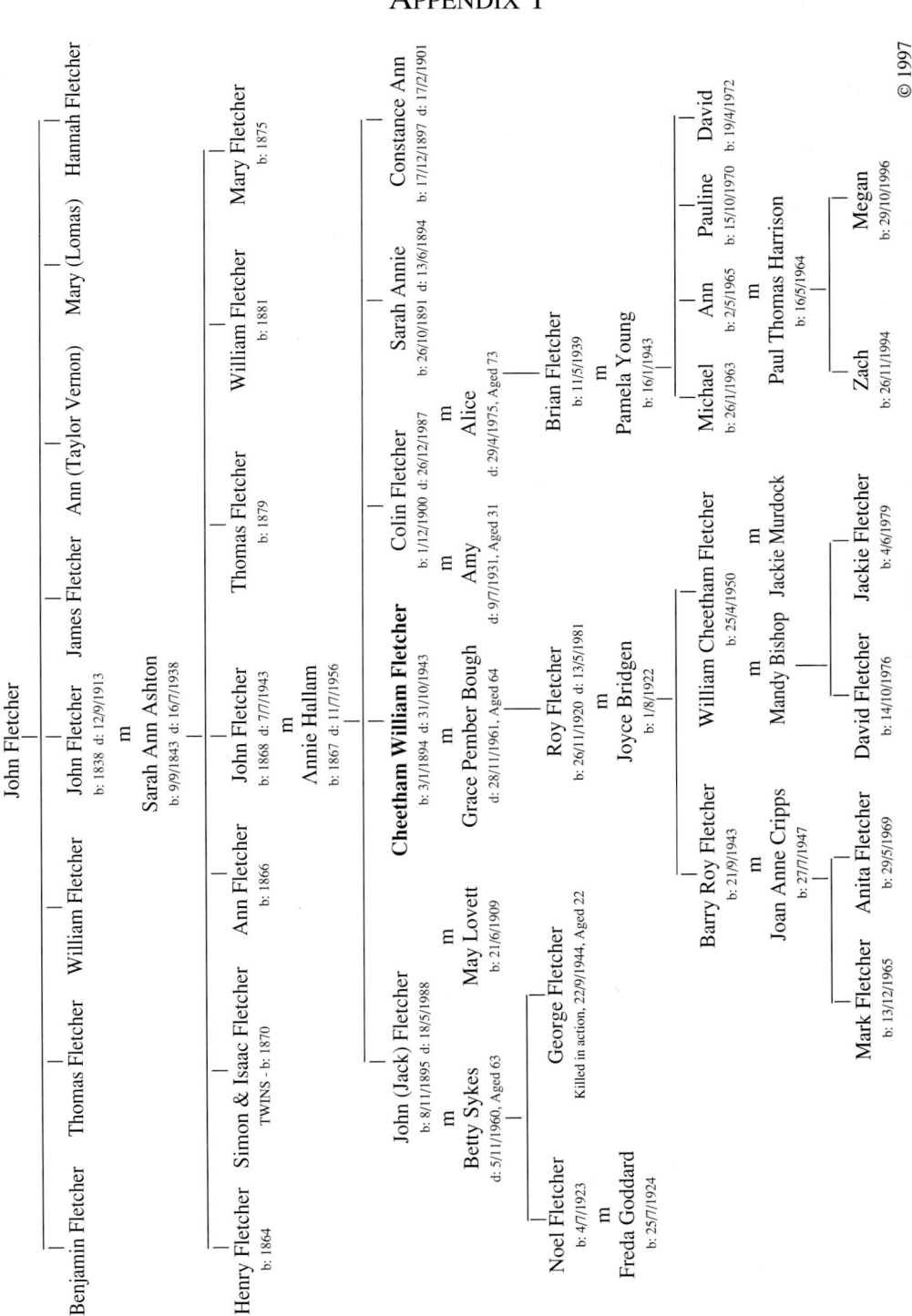

John Fletcher

- Benjamin Fletcher b: 1864
- Thomas Fletcher
- William Fletcher
- Henry Fletcher / Simon & Isaac Fletcher TWINS - b: 1870
- James Fletcher
  - m Sarah Ann Ashton b: 9/9/1843 d: 16/7/1938
  - John Fletcher b: 1838 d: 12/9/1913
- Ann (Taylor Vernon)
- Mary (Lomas)
- Hannah Fletcher

Children of John Fletcher & Sarah Ann Ashton:
- John Fletcher b: 1868 d: 7/7/1943
  - m Annie Hallam b: 1867 d: 11/7/1956
- Ann Fletcher b: 1866
- Thomas Fletcher b: 1879
- William Fletcher b: 1881
- Mary Fletcher b: 1875

Children of John Fletcher & Annie Hallam:
- John (Jack) Fletcher b: 8/11/1895 d: 18/5/1988
  - m May Lovett b: 21/6/1909
- **Cheetham William Fletcher** b: 3/1/1894 d: 31/10/1943
  - m Grace Pember Bough d: 28/11/1961, Aged 64
- Colin Fletcher b: 1/12/1900 d: 26/12/1987
  - m Amy d: 9/7/1931, Aged 31
  - m Alice d: 29/4/1975, Aged 73
- Sarah Annie b: 26/10/1891 d: 13/6/1894
- Constance Ann b: 17/12/1897 d: 17/2/1901

Children of John (Jack) Fletcher & May Lovett:
- George Fletcher Killed in action, 22/9/1944, Aged 22
- Betty Sykes d: 5/11/1960, Aged 63

Children of Cheetham William Fletcher & Grace Pember Bough:
- Roy Fletcher b: 26/11/1920 d: 13/5/1981
  - m Joyce Bridgen b: 1/8/1922

Children of Colin Fletcher:
- Brian Fletcher b: 11/5/1939
  - m Pamela Young b: 16/1/1943

Noel Fletcher b: 4/7/1923
  - m Freda Goddard b: 25/7/1924

Children of Roy Fletcher & Joyce Bridgen:
- Barry Roy Fletcher b: 21/9/1943
  - m Joan Anne Cripps b: 27/7/1947
- William Cheetham Fletcher b: 25/4/1950
  - m Mandy Bishop
- Jackie Murdock

Children of Brian Fletcher & Pamela Young:
- Michael b: 26/1/1963
- Ann b: 2/5/1965
  - m Paul Thomas Harrison b: 16/5/1964
- Pauline b: 15/10/1970
- David b: 19/4/1972

Children of Barry Roy Fletcher & Joan Anne Cripps:
- Mark Fletcher b: 13/12/1965
- Anita Fletcher b: 29/5/1969

Children of William Cheetham Fletcher:
- David Fletcher b: 14/10/1976
- Jackie Fletcher b: 4/6/1979

Children of Paul Thomas Harrison & Ann:
- Zach b: 26/11/1994
- Megan b: 29/10/1996

© 1997

Appendix 2

Sketch map of the Area

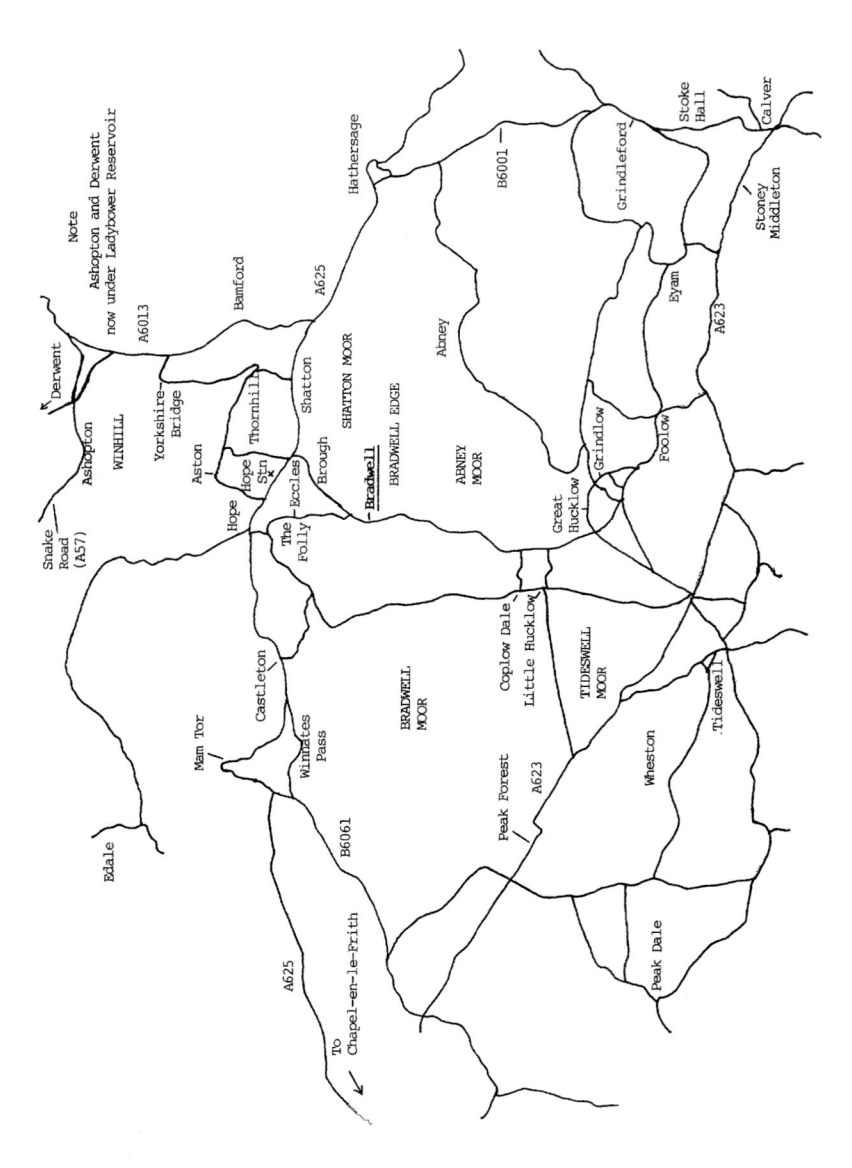

Appendix 3

Sketch map of the Village

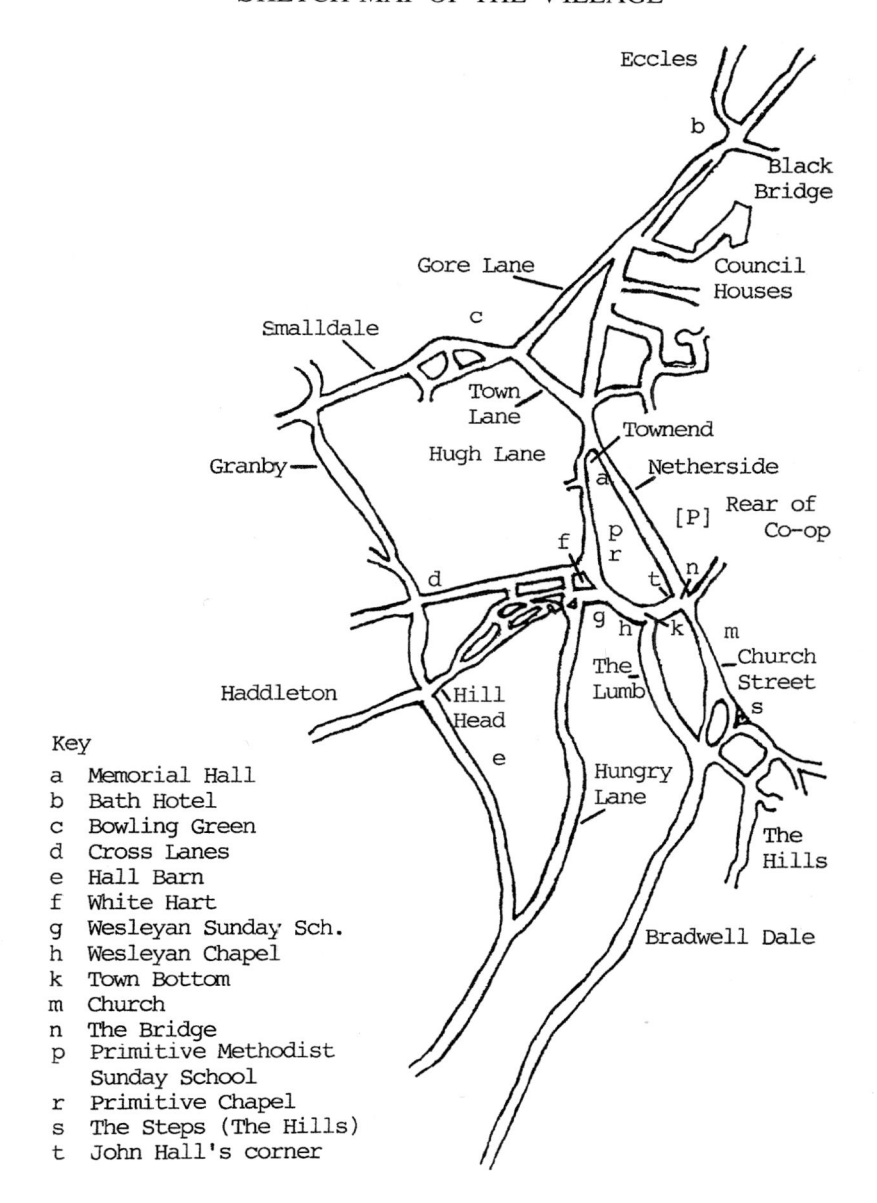

Key
a   Memorial Hall
b   Bath Hotel
c   Bowling Green
d   Cross Lanes
e   Hall Barn
f   White Hart
g   Wesleyan Sunday Sch.
h   Wesleyan Chapel
k   Town Bottom
m   Church
n   The Bridge
p   Primitive Methodist Sunday School
r   Primitive Chapel
s   The Steps (The Hills)
t   John Hall's corner

Walk One

The car park in Bradwell is situated behind the Co-op on the main road (Netherside). On leaving the car park cross the main road onto the opposite footpath and turn to your right. Proceed along the footpath until you reach the Post Office on your left. On the opposite side of the road are the extensive buildings of the Newburgh Engineering Company, a munitions works during WW2. Cheetham Fletcher was working here up until the time of his death, 31 October 1943. Continue along the footpath to the village Memorial Hall. This is where the Home Guard drilled and held lectures. Look to the right of the village hall entrance to see Townend. The property, two adjoining houses standing in a yard, is where Cheet' and Grace lived and the cottage on the left bears his name "Cheetham Cottage". The property is the birthplace of Cheet's two grandsons, Barry and Bill, and his great-grandson, Mark. On the opposite side of the road is a bungalow, set back and to the right of which is a large concrete block and wood building. This was Fletchers' workshop where Cheet' and brother Jack, and later their sons, worked in the family business.

Walk to the end of the footpath and cross Hugh Lane and Town Lane to rejoin the path at the rear of the big tree. As you continue along the path it is interesting to note that the properties to your right would not have been built during Cheetham's life. At the end of the path cross Gore Lane and rejoin the path just beyond the bus shelter. The entrance to the right of the bus shelter leads to Earl's, now Blue Circle plc. Pass this entrance, rejoin the footpath and continue to the Bath Hotel. The Home Guard sited a road block here and buildings to the rear of the public house were used as a HQ. The road to the left leads to Hope via Eccles. Opposite the Bath Hotel is a lane leading to Black Bridge, just past the new bowling green. Turn and retrace your steps to the bottom of Gore Lane.

Walk up Gore Lane to the top corner of the triangular field. From this point the walk climbs quite steeply so unseasoned walkers may wish to continue with walk two. If staying with walk one follow the road upwards, around the double bend and into Smalldale. Continue upwards, passing the Bowling Green Inn on your right. The two bungalows on the left are on the site of the original bowling green. Continue climbing until Granby Road on the left, recognised by railings at its start. Walk along Granby Road, from which there are magnificent views into the Hope Valley, until Cross Lanes with Charlotte Lane to the left and the track to Moorbrook on the right. Continue straight ahead until the next junction with Hill Head to the left and Haddleton to the right. A little way ahead, on the left, is Hall Barn (Old Barn) referred to by Cheet' in one of his ghost stories. Return to the cross-roads and proceed down Hill Head.

After a few metres the road forks. Take the right fork and walk down the hill, into Far Hill, and stop at the top of a footpath with steps. Turn to look back up Far Hill. To your right is Briar Cottage and beyond that is Rock Hill Cottage, which was probably Cheet's birthplace. The cottage on your left, Mountain View, was the home of Cheet' and Grace until 1933. To the left of this cottage, a private path leads to Hills View where Cheet's parents lived for many years.

Walk down the footpath with the steps, bear left onto Hollow Gate then turn right down the road to the White Hart public house on the left.

Opposite the White Hart is the Wesleyan Sunday School under which the Home Guard had its small bore rifle range. Below the Sunday School is a joiner's workshop and shop, beyond which are the gates to Bradwell Methodist Church. If you have time, a short walk up the drive, turning right just before the steps, will bring you in a short distance to the graveside of Cheetham William Hallam and his wife Sarah. Cheet's two sisters, Sarah Annie and Constance Ann were also buried in this graveyard.

Proceed down Town Gate to the bottom of the hill, this area being Town Bottom. Turn right and with Bradwell brook on your left follow the Lumb until the junction with the main road. The area in front of you is The Hills; the road to the right leads to Bradwell Dale. Turn left and walk down the footpath, passing the Valley Lodge public house (formerly the Shoulder of Mutton) until you see the Church on your right.

Looking into the churchyard you will see one grave with a square arch directly in line with the church tower: this is Cheet's grave. By entering the churchyard you will be able to spend time looking at the War Memorial and the graves of many of Cheet's close relatives. Within the Church is a wall plaque, depicting The Last Supper, which was given by Grace in Cheet's memory. Two processional crosses are in memory of Cheet's nephew (George) and Cheet's brother (Jack).

Leave the churchyard, turn right and follow Church Street to the bridge over Bradwell Brook. Look downstream to see the building spanning the brook in which Cheet's father started his business in the early 1900s. Continue your journey to arrive back at the car park near the Co-op. The length of this walk is a little under two miles.

Walk Two

The journey to the top of Gore Lane is exactly the same as for Walk One. Instead of proceeding up Smalldale, turn left down Town Lane and walk to the junction. Bear right into Hugh Lane passing the back of Cheetham Cottage and the rear of the Memorial Hall. Looking to your right notice the railings of one of the village schools, opened in the late 1890s and probably attended by Cheet'. Continue the gradual climb until the Primitive Methodist Sunday School building on the left, which became the home of the Mobile Guard (Home Guard) in May 1941. As the road levels you will see the Primitive Methodist Chapel building on your left, now in private hands. Keep left and walk down the hill to the White Hart public house. From the White Hart continue as for Walk One. The length of this walk is a little over one mile.

APPENDIX 4

List of key dates before, during and after Cheet's life

1838	John Fletcher born (Cheet's grandfather)
09 Sep 1843	Sarah Ann Ashton born (Cheet's grandmother)
1845	Cheetham W Hallam born (Cheet's maternal grandfather)
1848	Sarah born (Cheet's maternal grandmother)
1850	William Bough born (Grace's father)
1867	Annie Hallam born (Cheet's mother)
1868	John Fletcher born (Cheet's father)
26 Oct 1891	Sarah Annie Fletcher born (Cheet's sister)
03 Jan 1894	Cheetham William Fletcher born (Cheet')
13 Jun 1894	Sarah Annie Fletcher died (Cheet's sister) aged 2 years and 8 months
31 Jan 1895	Harry Bough born (Grace's brother)
08 Nov 1895	John (=Jack) Fletcher born (Cheet's brother)
29 May 1897	Grace Pember Bough born (Cheet's wife)
17 Dec 1897	Constance Ann Fletcher born (Cheet's sister)
01 Dec 1900	Colin Fletcher born (Cheet's brother)
17 Feb 1901	Constance Ann Fletcher died (Cheet's sister) aged 3 years and 2 months
12 Sep 1913	John Fletcher killed in accident (Cheet's grandfather) aged 75
07 Sep 1914	Cheet' enlisted with Sherwood Foresters
27 Feb 1915	Cheet' arrived in France
22 Aug 1915	Cheetham W Hallam died (Cheet's maternal grandfather) aged 70 years (buried Bradwell Methodist Church)
24 Dec 1915	Cheet' wounded in chest
22 Jan 1916	Cheet' arrived back in England
13 Jun 1916	Marriage of Cheet' to Grace Pember Bough (Bakewell Register Office)

15 Jun 1916	Cheet' returned to France and stayed until the end of the war
14 Feb 1920	Sarah Hallam died (Cheet's maternal grandmother) aged 72 years (buried Bradwell Methodist Church)
26 Nov 1920	Roy Fletcher born (only child of Cheet' and Grace)
01 Aug 1922	Leonora Joyce Bridgen born (Roy Fletcher's wife)
16 Jul 1938	Sarah Ann Fletcher died (Cheet's grandmother) aged 95 years (buried Peak Forest Church)
01 Aug 1942	Marriage of Roy Fletcher to Joyce Bridgen
07 Jul 1943	John Fletcher died (Cheet's father) aged 75 years (buried Bradwell C of E)
21 Sep 1943	Barry Roy Fletcher born (Cheet's grandson)
31 Oct 1943	Cheetham William Fletcher died aged 49 years (buried Bradwell C of E)
22 Sep 1944	George Fletcher killed in action (Cheet's nephew) aged 22 years (commemorated Bradwell C of E)
25 Apr 1950	William Cheetham Fletcher born (Cheet's grandson)
11 Jul 1956	Annie Fletcher died (Cheet's mother) aged 89 years (buried Bradwell C of E)
28 Nov 1961	Grace died (Cheet's wife) aged 64 years (buried Bradwell C of E)
31 Mar 1962	Emily Emelia Bough died (Grace's sister-in-law)
13 Dec 1965	Mark Barry Fletcher born (Cheet's great-grandson)
29 May 1969	Anita Joan Fletcher born (Cheet's great-granddaughter)
21 Jan 1970	Harry Bough died (Cheet's brother-in-law) aged 74 years

14 Oct 1976	David Fletcher born (Cheet's great-grandson)
04 Jun 1979	Jackie Fletcher born (Cheet's great-granddaughter)
13 May 1981	Roy Fletcher died (Cheet' & Grace's son) aged 60 years (buried Bradwell C of E)
26 Dec 1987	Colin Fletcher died (Cheet's brother) aged 87 years (buried Bradwell C of E)
18 May 1988	Jack Fletcher died (Cheet's brother) aged 92 years (buried Bradwell C of E)

APPENDIX 5

LIST OF ILLUSTRATIONS

Thanks are given for the loan of pictures to the people whose initials are shown in brackets:

Brian & Pam Fletcher (B&PF); Joyce Fletcher (JF); Sheila & Ned Fletcher (S&NF).

Frontispiece

	Page
Cheetham William Fletcher; circa 1938	iv

Chapter 1

John, Annie & family, Rock Hill cottage; circa 1900 (JF)	21
Cheet', Jack and Colin, Rock Hill cottage; circa 1905 (B&PF)	21
Dam Dale Farm, Peak Forest (S&NF)	22
John Fletcher's workshop at The Butts, Bradwell (JF)	25
Early Business Card - "Fletchers" (B&PF)	25
As a young man, Cheet' in Sunday best clothes; circa 1912	25
William Bough aged 52 years; 1902 (JF)	26

Chapter 2

Embroidered card to brother Colin (B&PF)	29
Grace with ornate window in background (JF)	30
Post Card from Grace to Cheet; September 1916 (JF)	30
Cheet' and army colleague in uniform, bareheaded	31
Cheet' with army colleague in Tin Hat	31
Cheet' with six army colleagues (B&PF)	31
Grace aged 18 years seated on wall; 1915 (B&PF)	32
Embroidered card to Annie (B&PF)	33

On Active Service Envelope to Annie (B&PF)	34
Front of 139th Infantry Brigade Christmas Card (B&PF)	36
Picture inside Christmas Card (B&PF)	36
Embroidered Card to Mother, Annie (B&PF)	47
Embroidered Card to brother, Colin (B&PF)	47
Embroidered Card to Annie (B&PF)	47
Cheet' in dress uniform	47
Good Wishes embroidered card to his mother (B&PF)	48
Brother Jack in Sherwood Foresters' Uniform	49
Grace's brother Harry (JF)	49
Grace in group outside the Bath Hotel (JF)	49
Mentioned in Despatches Certificate	54
Page 107 of Cheets's journal	58

Chapter 3

Seven young men enjoying a Sunday walk	70
The grave of Annie Fletcher's parents (B&PF)	73
Colin and Amy - early days (JF)	74
Jack and Betty - early days (JF)	74
Townend joiners' shop	75
Cheet' taking a short breather; July 1924 (B&PF)	75
Grandpa Fletcher & Grandson Roy; July 1924 (B&PF)	75
Cheet's uncle Bill in the wheelwrights' shop (S&NF)	75
Cheet's grandmother, Sarah Ann, of Peak Forest	77
Roy and grandpa John, Hills View; circa 1930 (B&PF)	78
Cheet', Grace, Roy & Lil outside Hills View; circa 1931	78
Cissy and Ernest Dungworth outside Briar Cottage	79
Drawing of Townend shop; circa 1934 (JF)	80
A smiling John Fletcher on his small farm (JF)	81
John Fletcher shooting (B&PF)	82
Grace outside Townend shop; circa 1936 (JF)	83
Cheet' & Grace, Monsal Head, Derbyshire; June 1929	84
Grace and Cheet' out for a stroll	86

Roy on holiday in Blackpool; circa 1938 (B&PF)	86
Cheet' & Grace on holiday, Blackpool; circa 1938	86
Colin with his second wife, Alice (B&PF)	86
All in a day's work (JF)	90
Working at the Snake Inn	90
Cheet' taking a well earned drink	90
Cheet' installing bells at St Barnabas Church; 1938	91
Cheet' during installation of bells; 1938	92
Cheet, Noel, Jack and Colin, Joiners' Shop; circa 1939	92

Chapter 4

Roy and Joyce - early days	133
Noel Fletcher (JF)	134
George Fletcher (JF)	134

Chapter 6

Roy and Joyce's Wedding Day; 1 August 1942	155
Roy and Joyce on their wedding day; 1942	156
Len and Florence together with Grace and Cheet'; 1942	156

Chapter 8

Annie Fletcher	170
Barry with Grace; circa 1949	173
Grace and her brother Harry; circa 1958	176

Appendices

Family Tree	187
Sketch map of the area	188
Bradwell Village map	189

APPENDIX 6

BIBLIOGRAPHY

CANEY, Robert S	"The Story of St Barnabas' Church, Bradwell"; printed by T W Warrington & Son Ltd, Tideswell; 1968
ENGLISH LIFE PUBLICATIONS	"The Sherwood Foresters - A Brief History"; "English Life Publications Ltd, Derby; 1980
EVANS, Seth	"Bradwell Lead Mining Customs"; in the Journal of the Derbyshire Archaelogical Society, Volume 33; 1911
EVANS, Seth	"Methodism in Bradwell"; 1907
HARRIS, Helen	"Industrial Archaelogy of the Peak District"; Ashbourne Editions, Ashbourne; 1992
HIBBERD, Dominic	"Wilfred Owen - The Last Year" Constable, London; 1992
LAFFIN, John	"Panorama of the Western Front"; Alan Sutton Publishing, Stroud, Gloucestershire; 1993
PRIESTLEY, Major R E; MC; RE	"Breaking the Hindenburg Line - The story of the 46th (North Midland) Division"; T Fisher Unwin Ltd, London; 1919

INDEX

Abney Moor; 150
Allen, C H; 127
Allen, C T; 127
Andrew, Charles; 13
Andrew, Clifford; 70
Andrew, C W; 127
Andrew, F; 127
Andrews, Dr Mary; 114-16
Applegate, PC; 78, 106
Arnhem; 172
Arnold, C E; 127
Ash, old Mr; 13
Ashbury, J; 93-105, 107-8, 114-15, 117-19, 121-2, 125-6
Ashby De La Zouch; 50
Ashmore, Albert; 70
Ashmore, H L; 127
Ashopton; 103, 125
Ashton, fish tenter; 15
Ashton, Sarah Ann; 22, 76, 187, 194
Aston; 101
Atkinson, R; 33
Backworth; 27
Baker, D R; 127
Bakewell; 157-158
Bakewell Register Office; 33, 45, 165, 194
Baldwin, 1st Lieut; 93, 97-101, 103-4, 106-9, 118-19, 122-3, 125
Bamford; 24, 83, 87, 89, 93, 95-9, 101-16
Bamford Church; 89, 114
Bamford Mill; 19, 24, 33, 63
Bamford station; 89
Bath seat, the; 18, 24
Bath Hotel; 96, 107-11, 117, 190
Bath Hotel, old; 24, 49
Belper; 50
Bennett, Mrs R; 110
Bennett, R; 128
Bessie Lane; 128
Bethlehem Chapel; 59
Bethlehem Church; 146
Black Bridge; 107, 190
Bossingham, Mrs; 110

Bottomley, I; 127
Bough, Barry; 177
Bough, Bill; 84-5, 87-8, 177, 181
Bough, Billy; 26, 84-5, 88
Bough, Cissy; 84, 87
Bough, Emily; 85, 89, 175, 195
Bough, Grace Pember; 24, 26, 29-30, 32-3, 187, 194
Bough, Harry; 26, 49, 84-5, 87, 89, 175-6, 194-5
Bough, Helen; 175
Bough, Jack; 83-5, 87-8, 174-5, 177
Bough, Roy; 84, 87
Bough, William; 26, 33, 89, 194
Bowling Green Inn; 107, 154, 191
Boyes, R; 120, 125
Bradwell Brook; 24, 131, 192
Bradwell, C; 94
Bradwell Church; 102, 132, 157-8, 192
Bradwell Church bells; 91-2
Bradwell Church school; 80, 168
Bradwell Churchyard; 24, 53, 148, 168, 192
Bradwell Cub Scouts; 24
Bradwell, Cyril; 116, 126
Bradwell, D; 128
Bradwell Dale; 13, 16, 96, 100, 103, 106, 116, 120-4, 132, 151-2, 192
Bradwell Edge; 82, 97, 118
Bradwell, H; 94, 103, 107, 113, 115, 118-19, 122
Bradwell, Hedley; 95, 116
Bradwell, H S; 126
Bradwell, Hugh; 120, 127
Bradwell, John; 17
Bradwell, L; 119, 122, 126
Bradwell, Leslie; 107
Bradwell Moor; 99
Bradwell, Mrs Albert; 59
Bradwell, Mrs Doug; 110
Bradwell, Percy; 27, 53
Bradwell Red Cross Unit; 116
Bradwell, William; 12
Bramall, David; 150
Bramall, Mrs Joe; 59

201

Brentwood Road, Bamford; 177
Bretton Clough; 124
Briar cottage; 34, 48, 79-80, 178, 191
Bridge, the; 14, 17, 24, 131
Bridge End; 126
Bridge Street; 129
Bridgen, Florence; 155-6
Bridgen, Joyce; 195
Bridgen, Len; 155-6
Bridgen, Len (Jnr); 155
Bridgen, Muriel; 155
Broadbent, D; 128
Bromage, Mrs; 110
Brook Buildings; 23, 128
Broom, Emily Amelia; 84, 87
Brough; 89, 98, 101, 104, 125, 127-8, 140-41, 148
Brough Lea Farm, Bradwell; 180
Brown, Bobby; 12-14, 23, 148-9
Brown, E; 102
Brown, Mr & Mrs; 88
Brown, T; 128
Bull Ring, the; 28
Bull's Head Hotel, Castleton; 108
Bull's Head, Little Hucklow; 131
Burgon, Sgt; 93
Burnstall Lodge Farm; 126
Burrows, 2nd Lt Leonard Victor; 42, 50
Burrows, A; 120, 128
Butts, the; 25, 73
Buxton Lime Firms; 20
Buxton, T R; 128, 131-2, 182
Carbolite Company; 24
Castleton; 13, 93, 95-6, 101-4, 108, 123-4, 149
Charles, R; 93-4, 126
Charlotte Lane; 191
Cheetham cottage; 70, 80, 85, 190, 193
Cheetham, William; 20
Church Street; 17, 23, 126-130, 182, 192
Coats Green; 113
Constitutional Club; 24
Cooke, S; 128
Cooke, Sewell; 89
Cooper, Bill; 64, 70

Cooper, Luther; 12
Cooper, T M; 128
Coplowdale, 103, 114-15, 118, 123, 131
Cravens of Darnall; 19, 24
Critchlow, H H; 126
Critchlow, William; 23
Crookhill; 97
Cross Lane Villas; 105
Crosslanes; 97, 108-110, 191
Cushworth, Dorothy; 82, 175
Cushworth, Wilf; 66, 70, 80, 82, 175
Dakin, Donald; 70, 128
Dakin, S A; 128
Dale End; 127
Dam Dale Farm; 22, 77, 165, 179
Daniel, A; 128
Daniel, E; 94; 126
Daniel, G; 94, 119-20, 126
Derby Barracks; 27
Derbyshire Courier; 32, 45
Derbyshire Records Office; 163
Derbyshire Times, the; 132
Derwent Arms, Bamford; 89
Derwent Church; 89
Derwent Reservoir; 26
Derwent Village; 26, 89, 102-4, 125
Dialstones; 24, 79-80, 126-7, 130, 154, 171, 180
Ditchman, A J; 128
Dixon, Jack; 18
Du Gard Peach, L; 100, 103-4
Dungworth, Cissy; 79, 178
Dungworth, Ernest; 79, 178
Dunn, James; 164
Dutton, R; 126
Earle, Mrs; 110
Earl's Cement; 85, 89, 94-5, 98, 103, 108, 110, 117, 119, 132, 171, 190
Easton, J V E; 126
Eccles; 100, 190
Edale; 104, 121-2
Edale Rifle Range; 120-21, 123
Elliott, Albert; 14
Elliott, Allan; 63
Elliott, Billy; 18
Elliott, Ernest; 131
Elliott, George (Bradwell); 151

Elliott, George (Little Hucklow); 151
Elliott, Marshall; 12, 71, 102
Elliott, T W; 128
Elliott, W; 128
Evans, Cyril; 14
Evans, Dennis; 18
Evans, Emma; 12
Evans, Len; 76, 82
Evans, Polly; 76, 82, 158
Evans, Seth; 20, 141
Eyam; 180
Eyre, B; 119-20, 126
Eyre, Bateman; 107
Eyre, Horace; 66
Eyre, R; 94, 101, 105, 119; 126
Eyre, Roy; 115
Far Hill; 11, 20, 24, 34, 48, 62, 72, 79, 129-30, 152, 191
Fathers, A; 122, 127
Fern Bank; 78
Fern, K; 122, 127
Fern, Kenneth; 107, 116
Fiennes, Mr; 117-19, 121, 125
Fischer, Miss; 110
Fischer, Mr; 146-7
Fischer, Mrs; 110
Flack, L; 128
Fletcher, Alice; 86, 154, 158, 171, 187
Fletcher, Amy; 74, 89, 187
Fletcher, Annie; 20-23, 33-4, 36, 47, 79-80, 130, 170, 195
Fletcher, Barry; 45, 157-160, 162, 173, 186-7, 190, 195
Fletcher, Benjamin; 23, 187
Fletcher, Betty; 154-5, 158, 171
Fletcher, Bill; 75, 159, 164, 178, 181, 190
Fletcher, Brian (Nat); 66, 171, 180-81, 187
Fletcher, Colin; 21, 23, 29, 46-7, 74, 80, 86, 89, 92, 128, 146, 154, 170-71, 183, 187, 194, 196
Fletcher, Constance Ann; 21, 23, 182, 187, 192, 194
Fletcher, Francis; 22, 23
Fletcher, George; 70, 78, 80, 88, 94, 120, 122, 126, 134, 171-2, 187, 192, 195

Fletcher, Grace; 34-5, 45, 48-9, 72, 76, 78-80, 82-9, 139, 154-8, 172-6, 178, 181-2, 190, 192, 195
Fletcher, Hannah; 23, 187
Fletcher, Jack; 21, 23, 35, 48-9, 73-4, 76, 78-80, 84, 92, 154-5, 158, 165, 170-72, 180, 187, 190, 192, 194, 196
Fletcher, Jackie; 164
Fletcher, James; 23, 187
Fletcher, Jim; 71
Fletcher, Joan; 185
Fletcher, John; 20-25, 32-3, 66, 73, 75, 78-82, 109, 155, 182, 187, 194-5
Fletcher, Joyce; 23, 26, 45, 76, 78, 133, 153-8, 174, 181
Fletcher, May; 76, 89, 165, 171-2
Fletcher, Ned; 22, 165, 179
Fletcher, Noel; 70, 73, 76, 82, 92, 94, 115-16, 120, 122, 126, 130, 134, 164, 171, 187
Fletcher, Pam; 66, 180-81
Fletcher, Roy; 70, 72, 75, 78, 80, 85-6, 89, 94, 115, 119, 126, 133, 153-8, 168, 174, 179, 181, 187, 195-6
Fletcher, Sarah Ann; 76-7, 195
Fletcher, Sarah Annie; 23, 180, 182, 187, 192, 194
Fletcher, Sheila; 22, 165, 179
Fletcher, Thomas; 23, 187
Fletcher, William; 23, 187
Fletcher, William Cheetham; 53, 162, 187, 195
Flintoft, Thomas; 102, 132
Flintoft, W; 128
Folly, the; 100
Foster, Tom; 28
Fox Lane; 129
Fox, Qtr Sgt; 93
Gibson, A; 128
Gill, Eric; 175, 179
Goodison, H A; 128
Gore Lane; 96, 100, 128-30, 190-91, 193
Grainger, M; 93-4, 107, 110, 118, 127
Granby Road; 191
Great Hucklow; 95

Greaves's Croft; 61
Green Lane; 82
Gregory, H; 128
Grindlow; 95
Gutter, the; 128
Haddleton; 82, 106, 109, 118, 130, 191
Haig, General Sir Douglas; 54, 166
Hall Barn; 60-1, 191
Hall, Lena; 17
Hall, Mrs L; 110
Hall, Mrs Rachel; 62, 152
Hall, R; 128
Hallam, A; 94
Hallam, Alf; 26, 76
Hallam, Arthur; 130
Hallam, Ben; 26, 76
Hallam, Bob; 76
Hallam, Cheetham William; 20, 72, 192, 194
Hallam, Joe; 14
Hallam, R; 128
Hallam, Sarah; 72, 192, 195
Hall's corner, John; 12, 24;
Hancock, A F Ltd; 110
Hancock's, Bamford; 87
Hart, H; 128
Hartle Moor Lane; 118
Hartle, Tommy; 70, 80
Hathersage; 101, 124-25, 186
Hawes, Alf; 33
Hawley, C; 94-5, 122, 127
Hayes, Mrs; 110, 116
Hayward, George; 59
Hazlebadge Hills; 95-6, 108-9, 111, 119, 121-3
Hibbs, Hannah; 11
Hill, Capt; 93, 97, 99, 102, 105-110
Hill Head; 12, 24, 33, 62, 69, 80, 127-9, 191
Hill, Henry; 17
Hills, the; 17, 62, 106, 127-30, 192
Hills Stile; 106, 110
Hills View cottage; 48, 78-80, 170, 183, 191
Hindenberg Line; 52
Hoare, J; 128
Hoare, J R; 128

Hodgkinson, H; 128
Hollow Gate; 14, 16, 106, 126, 128, 191
Holmes, Sgt George H; 42, 50, 160
Hope; 93, 96, 101-3, 116, 118, 131
Hope Bridge; 100
Hope Church; 101
Hope Station; 27, 88
Hope Valley; 84-85, 88, 113
Housley, Cliff; 45, 50
Howden reservoir; 26
Howe, H; 129
Howe, Harry; 88
Howe, John; 92
Howell, T; 129
Hugh Lane; 59, 117, 129, 154, 190, 193
Hungry Lane; 109, 148
Hunstone, Clarence; 33
Hyde, Cheshire; 164
Irongate; 129
Jacklin, E; 129
Jakeman; 93
Jeffrey Lane; 61, 128
Johnson, J; 129
Jones, E; 129
Jones, F; 129
Joyce, William; 130
Jungle, the; 27, 44
Kay, F; 129
Kiln Lane; 98
Knowles, James Henry; 66
Knowles, Jim; 64
Knowles, Ted; 59-60, 62
Ladybower reservoir; 26, 87, 89
Lakeman, 2nd Lt Reginald Noel; 42, 50
Lead mining; 140-41
Lee, H W; 129
Lewis gun; 103, 105, 107, 112, 117, 119, 121, 125-6
Little Hucklow; 15, 131, 151-2
Liverpool cathedral; 26
Liversedge, Frank; 13, 15
Liversedge, Mrs; 16
Liversidge, F P; 129
Local Defence Volunteers; 130
Lomas, Mary; 23, 187

Mabbott, Mrs H; 110
Maltby, Arthur; 13, 24, 41, 53
Mam Tor; 98, 102, 113, 115, 121
Marsden, W; 125, 129
Marshall, C; 127
Matlock; 163
McEntee, Dr; 150
McGibbons; 66
McKeen, Mr; 93, 104, 107, 109-12, 114-16, 126
McLellan, W H; 129
Memorial Hall; 60, 82, 87, 97, 99-108, 111-5, 158, 190, 193
Methodist Church, Bradwell; 23, 72-3, 175, 192, 194-5
Methodist Sunday School; 118
Mickelover; 28
Micklow; 70
Middleton, Dan; 66
Middleton, Eva; 70, 88
Middleton, Frances; 33
Middleton, Frank Roe; 13, 24
Middleton, G; 94, 127
Middleton, Hibbertson; 14, 16
Middleton, L E A; 168
Middleton, Lionel; 27, 53, 168
Middleton, nurse; 14, 16
Middleton, S; 129
Middleton, Sam; 70, 151
Middleton, Stephen; 106
Middleton, Vinny; 70
Millard, Mr; 106
Millard, Mrs; 110
Miller, H M; 128
Michlow Lane; 130
Monsal Head; 84
Moorbrook; 71
Morton, Miss Lily; 110
Mountain View cottage; 72, 78-80, 191
Mytham Bridge, Bamford; 83, 89, 175
Needham, Miss; 71
Netherside; 24, 127, 138, 157, 190
Newburgh, the; 138, 157, 190
New Church Street; 127
New Nook; 97, 127
Nicholson, F; 93-4, 104, 127
Nottingham; 50

O'Brien, T; 94, 127
Old Barn; 60-61, 191
Oldfield, Bill; 131
Oldfield, William; 14
Ollerenshaw, J C; 129
Outland Head; 129
Owen, Wilfred; 166
Palfreyman, Albert; 11
Palfreyman, Frank; 13
Palfreyman, John; 18
Paradise Farm; 127
Parritt, George; 78-9, 129-30, 178
Parsons Gate; 87
Pashley, Bill; 88, 127
Peak Advertiser, the; 163
Peak Forest; 19, 22, 23, 73, 75, 77, 82, 103, 163-5, 179
Peak Pavilion; 124
Pearce, Lt Arthur Carlton; 40, 50
Pember; 26
Philip, Mary; 63
Pindale; 151
Ponsonby, A; 129
Poole, G; 129
Poynton, Frank; 95
Poynton, J R; 129
Price, Lieut; 93, 98, 105, 107, 110, 118, 126
Primitive Chapel; 63
Primitive Methodist Chapel; 193
Primitive Methodist Sunday School; 117-9, 193
Quince, Albert; 65
Quince, Cyril; 106
Ramsdale; 120
Ramsdale, J W; 129
Repton, S; 129
Revell, Billy; 150
Revell, R; 94, 102
Revell, W (Jun); 94
Revell, W (Snr); 94
Revill, R; 115, 119, 122, 127
Revill, W C; 127
Revill, W H; 127
Rhodes, L/Cpl; 93
Rising Sun Hotel, Bamford; 175
Road Blocks; 96, 100, 105-6, 109, 119, 121-3

Roberts' bakehouse; 11, 23
Roberts, E; 93-4, 103, 105, 107, 115, 118-20, 125, 127, 129, 154
Roberts, G; 129
Robinson, A; 129
Robinson, L W; 129
Rock Hill cottage; 20, 21, 72, 191
Ross, Charles; 13, 24
Ross, Mrs; 16
Rowerth, Polly; 35
Rowland, A G; 127
Rowland, G; 120
Rowland, George; 116
Rowland, Mrs; 110
Rudd, J; 129
Sam, Sailor; 68, 70, 131
Sanderson, Mrs; 110
Saxon, G; 129
Seastron, Bill; 89, 131
Seastron, J W; 129
Senior, Fred; 64
Shatton Moor; 116
Sheffield; 24, 26-27, 29, 44, 61, 85, 88, 90, 104, 132-3, 149, 151-2, 161
Sheffield Star; 44, 157
Sheffield Telegraph; 44
Sheffield Town Hall; 26
Sherwood Foresters; 29, 33, 36, 44-5, 48, 50, 52-3, 160, 194
Shirley, old; 64-6
Shirt, Ben; 106
Shirt, Mr; 150
Shirt, W; 93-6, 103, 105, 108-11, 115, 118, 125, 127, 131-2
Simpson, Bill; 71-2
Skidmore, P; 94
Slag Works, the; 141
Slater, G; 130
Slater, George; 13
Smalldale; 12, 15, 71, 97-8, 106-7, 128-30, 191, 193
Smalldale Hall; 71
Smith, Marian; 165
Smith, Mrs Geo; 110
Smith, S S; 130
Smithy Hill; 127-30, 150
Snake Inn; 90
Southam, Pte F A; 50

Stoke Hall; 124
Stones, the; 66
Stoney Middleton; 131
Straw, G A; 130
Stretfield; 66, 127
Swindels, Shirley; 66
Swift, Bill; 12
Sykes, Betty; 35, 48, 74, 79, 187
Sykes, J W; 130
Tanks, tank traps; 112-13, 121, 123
Tants; 15
Taylor, A E; 130
Thacker, G; 93-7, 100, 105, 108-17, 120, 122-4, 127
Thompson, P; 130
Thornhill; 115, 185
Tideswell Moor; 96, 99
Tobin, M J; 130
Tommy Gun; 116, 120-21
Tor Top; 127
Towers, T F; 130
Town Bottom; 12, 17, 62, 78, 85, 131, 192
Town Gate; 23-24, 63, 72, 126-9, 192
Townend; 65, 70, 73, 75, 79-80, 82, 85, 88, 92, 126, 157, 171-2, 175, 190
Town Lane; 190, 193
Townsend, H F; 130
Travellers Rest; 101
Tynemouth; 28
Urwin, M; 130
Vernon, Ann Taylor; 23, 187
Vernon, Thomas Taylor; 23
Vernon, W; 99
Wain; 125
Wain, C; 93-4, 127
Walker, George; 13, 24
Walker, Mrs B; 110
Walker, Mrs Harry; 116
Walker, Wilf; 88
Walton, Mrs; 59
War Memorial; 24, 53, 168, 192
Weaver, A H; 130
Wesleyan School; 18, 20, 96
Wesleyan Sunday School; 101, 191
White, Annie; 180
White, Harry; 89, 130-131, 179

White, Raymond; 179
White Hart; 14, 63, 66, 191, 193
Whitley Bay; 27-8, 54
Williams, Bill; 65
Williams, E; 130
Williams, G; 120
Williams, George; 70
Williamson, I; 94, 127
Wilson, Jean; 70
Wilson, Jim; 66
Wilson, R; 94
Windy; 106, 118-20, 124, 130-31
Winhill; 96-7, 103, 109, 113, 117-8, 130
Winhill View, Bamford; 89, 175-6
Winkley, Elsie; 78
Wood, Ellen; 16
Wood, Mrs S; 110
Woodlands; 122
Wragg, John; 13
Wragg, Miss; 59-60
Wragg, Mrs B; 110
Yard End; 128
Yorkshire Bridge; 87, 89, 105

Be ever vigilant, But never Suspicious
Better to do well, Late Than Never
Birds of a feather flock Together
Better face a danger once Than be always
          in Fear.
By learning to Obey we know how to Command
Before you give way to Anger, Try to find a
      reason for not being Angry.
Beggars have no right to be Chusers
Better to be alone than in Bad Company
Better to be untaught than Ill Taught.
By a timely resistance the greatest evils
       may be Overcome
Begin nothing untill you have Considered
       how it is to be Finished.
Bad books are the public Fountains of Vice
Beware of him who regards not his Reputation
Bear and blame not what you cannot Change
Believe after Trial, and Judge before Friendship
Be Ashamed of your pride, Not proud of your Shame.
Be Slow to Promise, and Quick to Perform.
Beauty is the Flower, But Virtue is the Fruit of Life
Business makes a Man as well as tries Him
By Entertaining good thoughts, You will keep out
~~Candour and Op~~   Evil ones.
Candour and Open Dealing are The Honour of
~~Confine you~~   Mans Nature.
Confine your Tongue, lest it Confine you.
Contempt will sooner kill an Injury
        Than revenge